The Political Works of Remigius Dei Girolami

The Political Works of
Remigius Dei Girolami

Nicholas Newman

Saint Dominic's Media
Belleville, Illinois

Published by:
Saint Dominic's Media, Inc.
P.O. Box 8225
Belleville, IL 62222

www.saintdominicsmedia.com

Printed in the United States of America

19 29 21 22 23 24 25 8 7 6 5 4 3 2

BISAC Categories:
History / Europe / Italy
Philosophy / Political

ISBN-13: 978-1-7321784-5-8 (Paperback)
ISBN-13: 978-1-7321784-4-1 (Hardback)
ISBN-13: 978-1-7321784-3-4 (E-book)

Dedication

To my children: Orlando, Clayton, and Elisabeth, with all my love:

Remigius dei Girolami expounds on the importance of peace in the community. My hope is that you too remember the importance of peace amongst yourselves.

Contents

Contents

Contents

Contents

The General Introduction

Historical Background of Remigius' Works

As the lector of the Dominican *studium* in Santa Maria Novella[1] in Florence of the late thirteenth and early fourteenth centuries, Remigius dei Girolami was a witness to the Investiture Controversy, which was once a struggle between the Pope and the Holy Roman Emperor but had transitioned into being a conflict between the Guelfs and the Ghibellines and had gripped northern Itlay under a cloud of confusion.

I. The Investiture Controversy

I. That the Roman Church was founded by God alone...

III. That he alone may depose or reinstate a bishop...

---

[1] Davis (1960), 663. For more on Remigius dei Girolami's life and education see Davis (1960) and Panella (2014).

VII. That it is permissible for him alone to establish new laws, in times of necessity, to create new dioceses, to create an abbey of canons and to dissolve it, to divide a wealthy diocese and to unite poor ones.

VIII. That he alone can use the imperial insignia.

VIII. That the all princes ought to kiss the feet of the pope alone.

XII. That it is allowed for him to depose emperors.

XVIII. That his pronouncements can be repealed by no one, but he alone may repeal the pronouncements of any.

XVIII. That he himself may be judged by no one...

XXIII. That he may give permission and license for subjects to accuse their rulers...

XXV. That he may depose and reinstate bishops without the synod.

XXVI. That no one who does not conform to the Roman Church may be considered Catholic.

XXVII. That he can absolve subjects from their faithfulness to wicked rulers.[2]

The crux of Pope Gregory VII's (1075) position in *Dictatus Papae,* that the pope is the *locus* of both temporal

---

[2] Hofmann (1933), 202-208. I. Quod Romana ecclesia a solo Domino sit fundata... III. Quod ille solus possit deponere episcopos vel reconciliare... VII.Quod illi soli licet pro temporis necessitate novas leges condere, novas plebes congregare, de canonica abbatiam facere et e contra, divitem episcopatum dividere et inopes unire. VIII.Quod solus possit uti imperialibus insigniis. VIIII.Quod solius papae pedes omnes principes deosculentur... XII. Quod illi liceat imperatores deponere... XVIII. Quod sententia illius a nullo debeat retractari et ipse omnium solus retractare possit. XVIIII. Quod a nemine ipse iudicari debeat... XXIIII. Quod illius precepto et licentia subiectis liceat accusare... XXV. Quod absque synodali conventu possit episcopos deponere et reconciliare. XXVI. Quod catholicus non habeatur, qui non concordat Romanae ecclesiae. XXVII. Quod a fidelitate iniquorum subiectos potest absolvere.

and spiritual power to whom all other powers are subject, was in clear and forthright articulation on his view of the role of the Pope in the political landscape of Western Europe. It was this view that brought the conflict, which had been brewing between the Pope and the Holy Roman Emperor to a head.

Gregory VII, who was elected Pope in 1072, represented a victory within the Catholic Church for the "Gregorian Reformers,"[3] a group which wished to see moral reforms enacted within the Church, for example, the end of the practice of *simony*.[4] Published in 1075, the *Dictatus Papae* outlined, in twenty-seven principles, the powers he believed belonged to the Papacy. This attribution of powers to the Pope was not well received by the nobility, because they viewed it as being an infringement upon their power as rulers, and, thereby, making them in effect subject to the Roman pontiff allowing him to depose even the emperor as he willed. Such a view was especially true of the Holy Roman Emperor Henry IV (1056-1106), who responded to this text with a strongly worded letter calling for the Pope's resignation:

> Henry, the king not through usurpation but through the holy ordination of God, to Hildebrand, at present not pope but a false monk.
>
> Such greeting as this hast thou merited through thy disturbances, inasmuch as there is no grade in the church which thou hast omitted to make a partaker not of honour but of confu-

---

[3] These reforms are held in the *Dictatus Papae* of 1075, the *Register of Pope Gregory* of 1078 and the papal bull *Libertas Ecclesiae* of 1079.

[4] Discussed extensively in the *Register of Pope Gregory*. Cf. Gilchrist (1965) 209–235.

sion, not of benediction but of malediction. For, to mention few and especial cases out of many, not only hast thou not feared to lay hands upon the rulers of the holy church, the anointed of the Lord-the archbishops, namely, bishops and priests-but thou hast trodden them under foot like slaves ignorant of what their master is doing... Thou, therefore, damned by this curse and by the judgment of all our bishops and by our own, descend and relinquish the apostolic chair which thou has usurped. Let another ascend the throne of St. Peter, who shall not practise violence under the cloak of religion but shall teach the sound doctrine of St. Peter.[5]

The conflict between Pope Gregory VII and Henry IV did not stay in the realm of *Dictats* and letters but soon flared up even more with Gregory VII excommunicating Henry IV in 1076 and later deposing him. This was the spark that ignited the fifty years of civil war within the Holy Roman Empire, which was finally brought to an end with the *Concordat* of Worms in 1122, when the Holy Roman Emperor Henry V and Pope Calixtus II agreed that bishops and abbots owed their temporal authority to the king, but their spiritual authority to the pope:

I, bishop Calixtus, servant of the servants of God, do grant to thee beloved son, Henry-by the grace of God august emperor of the Romans-that the elections of the bishops and abbots of the German kingdom, who belong to the kingdom, shall take place in thy presence, without simony and without any violence; so that if any discord shall arise between the parties concerned, thou, by the counsel or judgment of the metropolitan and the co-provincials, may'st give consent and aid to

---

[5] Henderson (1910) 372-372

the party which has the more right. The one elected, moreover, without any exaction may receive the regalia from thee through the lance, and shall do unto thee for these what he rightfully should.[6]

In the name of the holy and indivisible Trinity, I, Henry, by the grace of God august emperor of the Romans, for the love of God and of the holy Roman church and of our master pope Calixtus, and for the healing of my soul, do remit to God, and to the holy apostles of God, Peter and Paul, and to the holy catholic church, all investiture through ring and staff; and do grant that in all the churches that are in my kingdom or empire there may be canonical election and free consecration.[7]

Neither side, then, had gained enough of an upper hand to force the issue entirely and because of this, there were periodic flare ups of this controversy. This is especially true in northern Italy, where the division between the emperor supported faction and the pope supported faction continued for several hundred more years.

II. Guelphs and Ghibellines

What sounds like the names of aliens on an episode of Star Trek, was a manifestation of the continuation of the Investiture conflict in northern Italy. The division between the Guelfs and the Ghibellines, who supported the Pope and Emperor respectively, dominated the politics of the northern Italian states until the fifteenth century.[8]

---

[6] Henderson (1910) 408-409.
[7] Ibid.
[8] Browning (1894) 192.

The presence of both the Guelf and the Ghibelline in Florence, left the city to be a site of continual conflict between the two factions. Under Frederick of Antioch, the Ghibellines controlled the city from 1244 to 1250, but the Ghibelline nobles attempted to broaden the social base of the government by including wealthy merchants. Through a policy called the *Primo Popolo*, these merchants were able to take power for themselves and Florence, thereby, became a Guelf city.[9] Guelf power suffered a setback after a defeat at the hands of the Sienese in the battle of Montaperti in 1260, after which the Ghibelline party was able to temporarily restore its power, thanks to the intervention of Pope Clement IV, who supported the Guelf faction.[10]

A short interlude in the Guelf vs. Ghibelline conflict, at least in the city of Florence, arose following the battle of Campaldino in 1289. The Florentine victory over the Ghibelline city of Arezzo in the battle assured Guelf supremacy in Florence.[11] It was not until 1325 that the Ghibellines were able to recover from this loss through the aftermath of the Battle of Zapollino, when the Ghibelline city of Modena was victorious and brought about a resurgence in Ghibelline fortunes.[12]

The Guelfs were not content to rest on their laurels after the downturn in Ghibelline power. Instead, they immediately split into two factions. The conflict between these two factions of the Guelfs, called the *Bianci* and the

---

[9] Najemy (2006), 68-71.
[10] This is discussed by Niccollo Machiavelli in his *History of Florence*.
[11] Browning (1894), 49 ff.
[12] Cf. Lenzi, (1995).

Neri, engulfed the city of Florence, as Dante discusses in Canto VI of the *Inferno*.

> Io li rispuosi: «Ciacco, il tuo affanno
> mi pesa sì, ch'a lagrimar mi 'nvita;
> ma dimmi, se tu sai, a che verranno
>
> li cittadin de la città partita;
> s'alcun v'è giusto; e dimmi la cagione
> per che l'ha tanta discordia assalita»
>
> E quelli a me: «Dopo lunga tencione
> verranno al sangue, e la parte selvaggia
> caccerà l'altra con molta offensione.
>
> Poi appresso convien che questa caggia
> infra tre soli, e che l'altra sormonti
> con la forza di tal che testé piaggia.
>
> Alte terrà lungo tempo le fronti,
> tenendo l'altra sotto gravi pesi,
> come che di ciò pianga o che n'aonti.[13]

The split between the two factions centered on the adoption of the Ordinances of Justice in 1293,[14] which the

---

[13] Dante *Inferno* VI 58-72. "No more he said, and I my speech resumed: "Ciacco! thy! dire affliction grieves me much, Even to tears. But tell me, if thou know'st, What shall at length befall the citizens of the divided city; whether any Just one inhabit there: and tell the cause, Whence jarring Discord hath assail'd it thus." He then: "After long striving they will come To blood; and the wild party from the woods Will chase the other with much injury forth. Then it behooves that this must fall, within Three solar circles; and the other rise By borrow'd force of one, who under shore Now rests. It shall a long space hold aloof Its forehead, keeping under heavy weight
The other opprest, indignant at the load, And grieving sore." Dante Alighieri *The Divine Comedy.* Henry F. Carey (trans.).

Bianci, the White Guelfs, under the leadership of the Cerchi family wanted to accept, while the *Neri,* the Black Guelfs, wanted repealed.[15] The Black Guelfs remained hardliners in their devotion to the Papacy, but the White Guelfs, as their opposition, maintained a more moderate outlook, and ultimately filled the vacuum of the anti-papal faction left by the downfall of the Ghibellines. The conflict grew to such an extent that it gave Charles of Valois a pretext for invasion in order to intervene between the two factions. This intervention tipped the balance in favor of the Black Guelfs, and prominent members of the White faction were targeted and exiled, such as Dante, who placed many of his enemies, among both the Ghibellines and the Black Guelfs, in the *Inferno.*[16]

III. Remigius Dei Girolami

It was in this context that the fundamental and often violent conflict between the White and Black Guelfs, which were destroying the very fabric of Florentine society, that Remigius, a Dominican friar attached to the Santa Maria Novella Church in Florence in the late thirteenth and early fourteenth century wrote his political treatises: *De Bono Communi* and *De Bono Pacis,* as well as his sermons on peace and his treatise *De Iustitia,* the texts presented in this translation.

A prolific author, Remigius published not only on political matters, but also on an impressive range of subjects from religious treatises such as: *Determinatio de Uno Esse in Christo, De Contrarietati Peccati* and *Contra Falsos Ec-*

---

[14] A series of statutory laws enacted against prominent Ghibbelines.

[15] Encyclopedia Brittanica *Vieri di Cerchi.*.

[16] Cf. Rupers (2016) for a list and description of these.

clesie Professores to scientific inquiries: *De Mixtione Elementorum Inmixto, De Modis Rerum* and *Divisio Scientie* and political treatises such as the *De Bono Communi* and the *De Bono Pacis.* While not a comprehensive list of his treatises,[17] this does give an impression of the breadth and scope of his writings.

He was also a highly educated and well-travelled scholar: "Remigio himself went at least twice to Paris and once to lecture on theology at the papal curia in Perugia."[18] Following his studies in Paris, he was made "lector of the Dominican *studium* in Santa Maria Novella."[19] Additionally, he received numerous other academic and religious offices, such as a *magisterium,* granted to him in 1302 as well as various administrative offices within the Dominican order.[20] Thanks to his learning and his position at Santa Maria Novella, Remigius was in a perfect position to describe and react to the political situation of Florence in the twelfth and thirteenth centuries and the effect that the Investiture Controversy had on the city, nevertheless, his work has garnered attention more for the illustrious names with whom he is connected than because of interest in his work. It was not until Charles Davis discussed his political theory in 1960 that an appreciation for his work, as such, developed.[21]

---

[17] See Davis (1960), 664 for a more exhaustive list of his works.

[18] Davis (1960), pg. 662.

[19] Davis (1960), 663.

[20] Cf. Davis (1960), 662-663 for a fuller biography of Remigius dei Girolami.

[21] Perhaps the single most influential Remigius scholar, however, is Emilio Panella, who not only edited many of Remigius' works, but done biographical and literary studies of Remigius as well.

Remigius was especially dependent upon the works of Thomas Aquinas,[22] which was understandable being that he was his pupil in Paris, and it was Aquinas who paved the way for the use of Aristotelian philosophy, as found in his *Commentaries on Aristotle* and in his *Summa Theologica*. It is interesting, however, that Remigius rarely mentioned Thomas Aquinas,[23] or refered directly to one of his texts.[24] It was not only in the use of Aristotle that

---

[22] The *Doctor Angelicus* of Medieval Scholastic Philosophy.

[23] In his *De Regno ad Regem Cypri* Thomas Aquinas discusses the merits (as well as the problems) of kingship, and lays out why the rule of one man is to be preferred over the rule of many (cf. Book I Caput III). This is problematic for the discussion in the *De Bono Communi* since Florence is a Republic. Aquinas does, however, discuss the issue of a benign monarchy (the best possible form of governance) degenerating into a tyrrany (the worst form) and points out the need for systems to be in place to guard against such a degeneration (Book I Caput VII). Not only does this imply limitations on the power of a king, an idea expounded on in the *De Iustitia,* but Aquinas allows for the commune itself to deal with the issue: Primo quidem, si ad ius multitudinis alicuius pertineat sibi providere de rege, non iniuste ab eadem rex institutus potest destitui vel refrenari eius potestas, si potestate regia tyrannice abutatur. Nec putanda est talis multitudo infideliter agere tyrannum destituens, etiam si eidem in perpetuo se ante subiecerat: quia hoc ipse meruit, in multitudinis regimine se non fideliter gerens ut exigit regis officium, quod ei pactum a subditis non reservetur. ("If to provide itself with a king belongs to the right of a given multitude, it is not unjust that the king be deposed or have his power restricted by that same multitude if, becoming a tyrant, he abuses the royal power. It must not be thought that such a multitude is acting unfaithfully in deposing the tyrant, even though it had previously subjected itself to him in perpetuity, because he himself has deserved that the covenant with his subjects should not be kept, since, in ruling the multitude, he did not act faithfully as the office of a king demands" [translation by Gerald Phelan]). In this case, the good of the *commune* is set even above the person of the king, as it is set above the individual members of the commune in the *De Bono Communi* and the *De Bono Pacis.*

[24] He does refer to Thomas Aquinas, for example, in *Quodlibet II* as: Magister meus quem sequor (my teacher, whom I follow). Friedman (2007). 430. Panella discusses the close relationship between the Christology and the understanding of form and unity displayed in the *Quodli-*

Remigius dei Girolami showed his reception of Thomas Aquinas. In the *De Iustitia*, for example, the understanding of the relationship of divine and human law, as well as the nature of virtue derive from Thomas Aquinas' understanding of these concepts in the *Summa Theologica*.[25]

The great reliance on Classical proofs and examples in the *De Bono Communi* is seen in the fact that references to Aristotle alone are used nearly as often as Scriptural references. In such pervasive use of Classical proof texts, especially the works of Aristotle, but also "Cicero...Virgil, Horace, Lucan, Ovid...Martial, Suetonius, Seneca Valerius Maximus, Aesop and Macrobius,"[26] Remigius showed his "breadth of ... reading" as well as his great love for the Classical world.[27] The Dominican was, of course, by no means unique in his use of the Classics. Petrarch, writing only shortly after Remigius, asked, "What is history, but the praise of Rome?"[28] Medieval intellectuals,[29] such as Paul the Deacon, John of Salisbury[30] and Godfrey of Fontaines,[31] as well as politicians, such as Arnold of Brescia,

---

beta of Remigius dei Girolami and Thomas Aquinas in the introduction to his edition of the *Quodlibeta* (Panella (1983). 35-42). Davis (1960), 663 too, mentions the close association of Remigius dei Girolami and Thomas Aquinas: "called St. Thomas 'the light of our eyes and the crown of our head;' two of the Angelic Doctor's sermons are included among his own works." This relationship is more difficult to pinpoint in Remigius' political works, but the dependence on Aristotle, at least, seems to come from his knowledge of the works of Aquinas.

[25] See below in the introduction to the *De Iustitia*, 188-194.
[26] Davis (1960), 665.
[27] Ibid.
[28] Davis (1974), 30.
[29] Cf. also Smalley (1971), 165-194.
[30] Among many others.
[31] Who also uses Aristotle in his discussion of property rights, c.f. Mäkinen (2011), 131.

also used Classical examples in their writings and to further their agendas.[32]

Remigius Dei Girolami's General Political Stance

I. The Good of the Community: A Global Problem as a Local Problem

In his discussion on the works of Remigius dei Girolami, Davis says: "Only by a rather extended analysis can one hope to do justice to the subtleties of his doctrine of the *potestas indirecta* and to recognize, without exaggerating its final inconclusiveness."[33] It is precisely this inconclusiveness that allows Remigius to tackle the issue of the division in Florentine society between the White and Black Guelfs. He does this in a radically different way than some of the others who write on this subject, Dante and Marsilius of Padua, for example, who suggested a division between temporal and spiritual power in the person of a king in their texts *De Monarchia* and *Defensor Pacis*.[34] Rather than call for further division, Remigius takes up the idea of the *bonum commune* from Thomas Aquinas,[35] whose *Summa Theologica* seems to serves not only as a theological but also a stylistic *hypotext* for Remigius.

---

[32] Ibid.
[33] Davis (1960), 672.
[34] Cf. Lee (2008). The relationship between the works of Dante and those of Remigius dei Girolami is discussed in Davis (1965), 415-435; Davis (1984) and Davis (1959) as well as in Minuo-Paluello (1956).
[35] Mineo (2014), 7.

Remigius is not shy about pledging his allegiance to the Papacy in other works,[36] but rather than placing blame for the issues plaguing Italy at the door of the pope and the emperor and having to choose between the two for a solution, the focus on the *bonum communi* allowed for a shift in the political narrative. Remigius never once mentioned the political parties of the Ghibellines and the Guelfs, or any members of these parties by name, as opposed to Dante who gleefully puts members of the Black Guelfs into his *Inferno*. Rather, he begins his *De Bono Communi* with the idea that this global issue is, at heart, not the fault of global forces clashing. Instead, this is the fault of the individual member of the commune putting his own personal and local interests above those of the commune at large.

> The prophecy of the apostle Paul in II *Timothy* says that: 'there follows close a perilous time, and there will be those who love themselves, who are greedy, puffed up and proud etc...' this is seen clearly fulfilled in these times and in modern men (alas, most of all in us Italians); who, because of their very great and inordinate love for themselves have neglected the good of their communities, because they have little or no care for them and, driven on by a demonic spirit, have thrown the castles, cities, provinces and the entire region into confusion through strife and destroyed them by assault.[37]

---

[36] Cf. his emphasis on the power of the pope in the *De Bono Pacis* V below, as well as his explicit support for the claim that "as far as the sun surpassed the moon in brightness so far did the Pope surpass all other rulers." Davis (1960), 671 quoting the *Contra Falsos Ecclesie Professores*.

[37] I. Prophetia beati apostoli Pauli, qua dixit II *Thim.* 3[,1-2] «Instabunt tempora periculosa et erunt homines se ipsos amantes, cupidi, elati, superbi» etc., hiis temporibus aperte videtur impleta in modernis hominibus et heu maxime in ytalicis nostris; qui quidem, propter nimium amorem

By opening his text with reference to II Timothy 3, which references the coming *Parousia,*Remigius immediately made clear the magnitude of the crisis. The individual, then, who put their own interests ahead of those of the larger community, is complicit not only in the destruction of that community but in the very end of the world. How, though, can the selfishness of the individual lead to such utter catastrophe? This comes about through Remigius dei Girolami's understanding of how the individual relates to the community as a whole:

> This follows secondly, since the existence of the part, such as it has, depends on the existence of the whole. The part existing beyond the whole is no longer a part, as it was called while it was part of the whole. The hand, when cut off, is not a hand, except ambiguously, just as, for instance, stone or painted ones, as is made clear by the Philosopher in book two of On the Soul, in book eight of the Metaphysics and in book one of the Politics; the hand does not have the ability to operate independently, for example to sense what is being touched, to bring food to the mouth, to cut and other such things.[38]

---

atque inordinatum sui ipsorum bona comunia negligentes, parum vel nichil de ipsis curando, spiritu diabolico agitati, castra civitates provincias totamque regionem hostilitatibus inordinatis confundunt et destruunt incessanter.

[38] IX. Secundo quia ipsum esse partis quale habet, dependet ab esse totius.Pars enim extra totum existens non est pars sicut prius dicebatur dum esset in toto. Manus enim abscisa non est manus nisi equivoce, puta sicut lapidea aut depicta, sicut patet per Philosophum et in II *De anima* et in VII *Methaphisice* et in I *Politice*; non enim habet operationes manus, puta sentire tangibilia, cibum ori porrigere, scalpere et huiusmodi.

Here, Remigius shows his dependence on the philosophy of Thomas Aquinas, both in the reliance on the authority of Aristotle, who is referred to more in the *De Bono Pacis* than Scripture is, and in the discussion of the relationship of the part to the whole.[39] For Thomas Aquinas, the existence (esse) of a part is dependent on the whole, "the esse of the concrete part just is part of the esse of the whole,"[40] and Remigius works within this understanding of the whole and the part:

> The relationship which the part has with itself is caused by the relationship which the part has with the whole, and it is preserved by this since the part, beyond the existence of the whole, does not exist, as is seen from what was said before.[41]

In applying this principle to the context of the Guelf/Ghibelline conflict, however, Remigius interprets the citizen of Florence is a part of a larger whole, the whole being the commune, as more defining of their identity than their own identity as an individual. If, then, the individual Florentine is a part of a greater whole, on which he depends for his very existence, then the apocalyptic destruction of the whole, of the "castles, cities, provinces and the entire region" is not merely an existential threat for the city, but for each individual living in that community: "Where, therefore, can the citizen or the Christian be beautiful with the flower of prosperity if his city or the church is withered, oppressed, destroyed? This

---

[39] Cf. Aquinas *Quodlibet* 9.3.
[40] Cross (2002), 53.
[41] X. Sed coniunctio quam habet pars ad se ipsam causatur a coniunctione quam habet pars ad totum, et conservatur ab ipsa quia pars extra totum existens non est pars, ut patet ex dictis.

is not possible. A flower is beautiful in the meadow, not in the dung or in the manure pile."[42]

All this seems a bit theoretical, however, and the Florentine citizen who is listening to a sermon by Remigius based on this text, or reading the text itself, may understand themselves as a member of a larger commune, and that they do depend on the commune in a general sense, but the Dominican insists that this dependence is not a general one, but transcends every aspect of the life of the citizen:

> Because of the destruction of the state the citizen remains as if stone or painted, since he lacks the operation and virtue which he had before: the soldier in military matters, the merchant in selling, the artist in the carrying out of his art, the official in his office, the head of the family in his family affairs and the universally free man in his freedoms, that is in going to visit his holdings, in making embassies, in having dominion over foreign cities and suchlike.[43]

The citizen of a commune is like a painting or statue, beautiful in the context in which it is supposed to be, and if the context in which the citizen has a good life and is able to perform those functions necessary to the carrying out of his work and life is destroyed, then the individual is destroyed along with it.

---

[42] IX. Quo igitur flore prosperitatis poterit pulcher esse civis vel christianus si sua civitas vel ecclesia sit exflorida, sit oppressa, sit destructa? Absit. Flos enim pulcher est in prato non in fimo vel sterquilinio.

[43] IX. Unde destructa civitate remanet civis lapideus aut depictus, quia scilicet caret virtute et operatione quam prius habebat, puta miles in militaribus, mercator in mercationibus, artifex in artificialibus artis sue, officialis in officialibus, pater familias in familiaribus, et universaliter liber in operibus liberis, puta ire ad podere suum, facere ambasciatas, habere dominia aliarum civitatum.

Despite the way in which the work opens, giving the reader, or listener, a particular setting: "in modernis hominibus et heu maxime in ytalicis nostris," the remainder of the text is curiously lacking in such specifics, and the follow up text to the *De Bono Communi*, the *De Bono Pacis* is also very generally written and never once mentions Italy or Florence specifically. What, however, does such generality bring to a text like this, and why does Remigius break from this pattern at certain points? This work was not written from the perspective of a Guelf or Ghibelline in order to attack the opposing side, nor is he airing grievances for attacks that he has endured himself, instead, he offers a road to reconciliation without necessarily compromising one's position, by always putting the interests of the commune, the community, above one's own.

By keeping to a general discussion, Remigius dei Girolami avoided controversy and creates a universally acceptable path to peace; this allowed him to address divisions in Florentine society other than the Black Guelf and White Guelf divide. For example, there was the constant struggle in the city by various families and factions for economic power as well.[44] The generality also poses a problem, however, as the danger exists that the text will be treated as a philosophical exercise, an intellectual discussion of how some individual fits into a larger community. This declawed the argument, and in order to mitigate this, and to bring a sense of urgency back into the text, the two instances in which he does reference the

---

[44] Davis (1960), 667.

city of Florence itself, the imagery is powerful. The first of these references is from chapter nine:

As he who was a Florentine citizen, because of the destruction of Florence is no longer to be called a Florentine, but rather a weeper. And if he is not a citizen he is not a human, since a human is naturally a political animal, following what the Philosopher says in book eight of the *Ethics* and the first book of the *Politics*.[45]

This passage is the culmination of a lengthy discussion of the interaction between the whole and the part, and how the individual citizen acts as a part of the whole of the community. All the theoretical and intellectual issues deriving from a breakdown in the commune, in the whole, are not just that, they have real consequences for the citizens of Florence, the destruction of their identity as a human.

In Section 13 of the *De Bono Communi*, Remigius discusses the way in which bodily attraction and the desire for beauty leads the individual to love the city more than himself, since the context of the city as a whole is more beautiful than the individual who is a part of it, since beauty is a matter of context, since beautiful things can look ugly outside of their proper context and ugly things can add to the beauty of the whole, as long as they play their proper role in the whole. Here again, the theoretical nature of the discussion proves a detriment to the conciliatory nature of the work, and so another discus-

---

[45] IX. Ut qui erat civis florentinus, per destructionem Florentie iam non sit florentinus dicendus sed potius flerentinus. Et si non est civis non est homo, quia homo est naturaliter animal civile, secundum Philosophum in VIII *Ethicorum* et in I *Phisicorum*.

sion of the direct impact of the dissolution of the whole commune has on the individual part that is the citizen:

> What kind of pleasantness can the Florentine citizen have, seeing the sad state of his city, filled with greatest sorrow? For the plazas are deplazad, that is they are emptied; the house is destroyed, the families are battered; the kinfolk are estranged; the comforts are discomfited; the games seem to have been played, that is lost; the dignities seem resented, that is by the statesmen and captains who have left the city; the offices seem bewitched, that is under a spell, the priory, the embassies and suchlike; the farms are laid waste, since the trees are torn out, the vines are cut down, the palaces are destroyed and it is not possible, that is one cannot, live in them any more or go to them without fear and trembling.
>
> Finally, the flower is wilted and the scent of fame is turned into the horrible odor of infamy, this fulfills the prophecy of its own name among the vulgar people, for they do not call it "Fiorenza" as foreign people do, but "Firenze." The French, when they come across dung, or some other fetid thing, they say: "fi fi" holding their nose, as if to say: "O how much this stinks!" Thus Florence is changed into Flerence, the city of tears. Therefore every citizen weeps because of natural love for Florence.[46]

---

[46] XIII. Qualem enim delectationem poterit habere civis florentinus videns statum civitatis sue tristabilem et summo plenum merore? Nam platee sunt explatiate idest evacuate, domus exdomificate, casata sunt cassata, parentele sunt exparentate, solatia sunt insollita, ludi videntur lusi idest perditi, dignitates videntur indignate idest potestarie et capitanerie que egrediebantur de civitate, officia videntur affacturata idest fascinata, scilicet prioratus, ambascerie et huiusmodi, poderia videntur expoderata quia arbores evulse, vinee precise, palatia destructa, et non est iam podere, idest posse, ut in eis habitetur vel eatur ad ea, nisi cum timore et tremore.

Both of these sections stand out from the rest of the text Not only because they are the only places which discuss Florence specifically, but also because they are the only places in which the author becomes playful with his language, using the similar sounds of Florentia, flerens, florens etc... to underscore to the listener the degeneration of Florence and the destruction of the whole.

II. A Global Solution to a Local Problem

In these texts, then, what is ultimately the clash of global powers has been reduced to the local level, to a problem with the whole of the commune, plagued by individuals putting their own goods over that of the whole. The cure for this malady is relatively simple, begin putting the good of the community before one's own, and a good percentage of the text is devoted to giving examples from, among others, from antiquity and from Scripture which illustrate how to put the state above one's own interests. In chapter IV, Remigius adds examples of creatures who have "natural love" i.e. animals. Especially striking is the discussion of how bees are preeminent in putting the good of the many over their own good:

> And again: there is no indolence found in the bee, no matter how close the examination; certain ones contend against other bees in the open, as if in war, others stand guard around

---

Denique flos exfloritus est et odor fame ipsius conversus est in horribilem fetorem infamie, iuxta prophetiam appellationis vulgaris civium: non enim "Fiorença", ut persone extranee, sed "Firençe" ipsam appellant. Gallici enim quando fimus vel aliquid aliud fetidum transit dicunt «fi fi» obturantes nares suas, quasi dicant «O quantus fetor est iste!». Et sic Florentia mutata est in Flerentiam. Quilibet ergo civis ex naturali amore ad Florentiam naturaliter habet flere.

their livelihood, others spy the coming rains and seek their coming together, others create wax out of flowers, others put together cells, some round and some segmented marvelous in their connection and similarity. Even in the midst of so much different work, not one is taken in ambush by another's labors, not one searches for food in order to take it, but after flying closer and working among the herbs and flowers, which are their own, he recovers and seeks harmony. The same person says that they set up a king for themselves whom they hold dear out of natural condition and whom "they defend to the highest degree and for whom they believe to die is glorious," because it is clear that the king is their head and rules the whole multitude.[47]

It is in this same context, examples of those who put the community above themselves, that Remigius took the opportunity to make one of his very few direct attacks on those he sees as not putting the community above themselves: "These men did not rob the community for their own gain, as do the officials in our own time; for the officials of the community, because they were poor before, are seen enriching themselves without any artifice in of-

---

[47] IV. Et iterum: in apum vero examine nulla est otiosa; quedam enim certant quasi in bello campestri contra alias apes, alie invigilant circa victum, alie futuros explorant hymbres et speculantur concursus, alie ceras de floribus fingunt, alie cellulas nunc rotundas nunc quadras mira connexione et equalitate componunt. Et tamen inter tam diversa opera nulla alienis laboribus insidiatur, nulla raptu victum querit, sed proprio volatu et labore inter herbas et flores que sibi sunt congrua recolligit et requirit. Item dicit quod constituunt sibi regem quem naturali affectu diligunt et «summa defensione defendunt et pro eo perire pulcrum putant», quia scilicet rex est earum caput regens totam multitudinem.

fice; this is certainly a most terrible sign."[48] In the *De Bo-no Pacis* he continues the discussion begun in the *De Bo-no Communi*, but does create a more specific recipe for creating peace in the city and in doing so moves from a personal level to the level of the community:

> It has been asked whether, for the good of peace and for the concord between cities and castles and other communities, wrongs and injuries that have done to us can be forgiven and if we can receive the same from other communities for the sake of unity among them all. It has also been asked whether this can be done without the assent of each individual person of those cities or communities, or even more against the will of any of those persons who have suffered wrongs and injuries, even those affiliated with the church.[49]

Not only is peace in the *commune* restored through the various individual parts putting the good of the whole above their own, but the whole can also act on its own and compel the individual parts to put aside their differences and to reconcile.

The general nature of the text being meant to allow for reconciliation within the community of Florence,

---

[48] V. Isti non abstulerunt comuni ut sibi acquirerent, sicut faciunt officiales moderni temporis; inveniuntur enim officiales comunis sine omni artificio in officio ditati, cum essent pauperes prius; quod certe pessimum signum est.

[49] I. Queritur utrum pro bono pacis et concordie inter civitates et castra et alias comunitates possit fieri remissio iniuriarum et dampnorum illatorum et receptorum per ipsas comunitates ad invicem componentes sine assensu omnium personarum particularium illius civitatis seu comunitatis, immo contra voluntatem aliquarum personarum passarum iniurias et dampna, etiam ecclesiasticarum.

Remigius did not often look outside of the *commune*, except as part of the paradigm of the part and the whole:

> From this undoubtedly follows that any citizen should prefer the common good of the city over his own good and any Christian the common good of the universal church over his own private good, since the total beauty of a part, in however many parts it is, depends on the beauty of the whole.[50]

Here, the Christian is discussed as part of Christendom in the same way that the citizen is a part of the community and hints at a progression of communities, this progression is made clear in chapter II:

> The Philosopher says in the first book of the Ethics: "though, indeed, good is the same both for an individual and for a community, it is better and more perfect to support and save a community; it is certainly pleasant for one person, but truly more divine for whole peoples and nations" i.e., for the many. This is as if he said that however much good is in common so much more is it to be loved, that is, the good of a city is more than the good of a private citizen and the good of a province, which contains many cities, more than the good of one city. From whence also and as a consequence the good of a kingdom is more to be loved than the good of a province and the good of the universal church more than the good of one kingdom.[51]

---

[50] IX. Ex quo indubitanter sequitur quod quilibet civis debet preferre bonum comune civitatis bono proprio et quilibet christianus bonum comune ecclesie catholice bono suo privato, quia tota pulcritudo partis in quantum pars est, dependet a pulcritudine totius.

[51] II. Dicit enim Philosophus in I *Ethicorum* «Si enim est idem bonum uni et civitati, maiusque et perfectius quod civitatis videtur suscipere et salvare; amabile quidem enim et uni soli, melius vero et divinius genti et civitatibus» scilicet multis. Quasi dicat: Quanto bonum est comunius tanto est magis amandum, scilicet bonum civitatis magis quam bonum unius

Like the individual is a part of the whole commune, so the commune is a part of larger whole, etc... and in the same way that the individual must put the good of the commune above his own, the commune must put the good of these larger entities above itself. Interestingly, this aspect of the argument, a logical continuation of the idea that the part is less than the whole, is not followed up on in the text, at least in the *De Bono Communi* and the focus remains mostly on the relationship of the citizen with their immediate community. In the *De Bono Pacis*, however, the idea of this progression is more developed, especially in terms of the power of the Papacy:

> Therefore, the good of the church relies on the peaceful union of the faithful, just as the Collect says: "those to whom you gave faith You also gave peace;" another states: "Your church, brought together by the Holy Spirit, is troubled in no way by attacks." Acts of the Apostles also says: "the church was enjoying peace throughout Judea." Judea can be interpreted as meaning "confessing," since it can refer to the confession of faith. In first Corinthians and in second Corinthians: "to the church of God which is in Corinth etc... grace and peace be with you." The ecclesiastical good is to be preferred over the temporal good, just as the head of the church, that is the pope, is to be preferred over the head of the temporal power, that is, over the emperor.[52]

---

civis et bonum provincie que multas continet civitates magis quam bonum unius civitatis. Unde et per consequens bonum regni magis amandum est quam bonum unius provincie et bonum universalis ecclesie magis quam bonum unius regni.

[52] V. Et ideo bonum ecclesie consistit in pacifica fidelium unione, sicut dicit collecta «Quibus dedisti fidem largiaris et pacem»; et alia «Ecclesia tua Spiritu sancto congregata hostili nullatenus incursione turbetur». Et *Act.* 9[,31] dicitur «Ecclesia per totam Iudeam pacem habebat». Iudea

This is one of the few places where Remigius let his true feelings on the Investiture controversy shine through; that the church, the papacy is the highest community of which all other communities are a mere part, and should love more than they love themselves. It is especially in the ninth sermon on peace, however, that the strongest stance is taken on the part of the Church: "Therefore bishops are good rulers, and above kings, as blessed Ambrosius is said to have spoken to Theodosius the emperor: 'In the church I am the lord, and you are as one of the common people.'"[53]

He wrote this passage in the context of a reconciliation between the clergy of Florence and the Dominican order, rather than directly in the context of the conflict of the Guelfs and Ghibellines, this statement seems to go beyond the question of whether the emperor or the pope is superior and puts the power solely in the hands of the clergy, that all bishops are superior to kings. The use of the Ambrosius quotation, however, returns Remigius to his ambivalence on this question due to the bishop being superior to the emperor in the church, it, thereby, implies that outside of the church the emperor is superior.

This same ambivalence is seen in the treatise *De Iustitia*: "As to the first, however, the two first precepts of justice pertain to the law; positive law too is double, that is divine and human and thus is double justice. Divine law

---

enim interpretatur confitens, quod ad confessionem fidei potest referri. Et I *Cor.* et II *Cor.* 1 «Ecclesie Dei que est Corinthi etc. gratia vobis et pax». Bonum autem ecclesiasticum prefertur bono temporali, sicut et caput ecclesie idest papa prefertur capiti temporalium idest imperatori.

[53] Bene ergo reges sunt episcope, immo et super reges; unde et beatus Ambrosius legitur dixisse Theodosio imeratori 'In ecclesia ego sum dominus et tu es sicut unus de plebe.

too is double, that is old and new. Human law too is double, that is civil and ecclesiastical. Civil law too is double, that is imperial and municipal."[54] Here again, the temporal and ecclesiastical authority is put on the same authoritative level, although the temporal authority is divided between the emperor and the municipality, reflecting on Remigius most comprehensive political work, *De Bono Communi*, in which the common good, the municipality, outweighs the individual, while the ecclesiastical authority is undivided.

III. Conclusion

It is by making the local become the global, generalizing his political treatises so that the focus is on the commune and its relationship with the individual parts that make it up, Remigius dei Girolami creates a text with which to heal the divisions in the city, rather than call for the victory of one side over the other. The danger of such a text becoming almost a philosophical exercise, rather than calling for true healing, is mitigated by periodically calling the city of Florence and her deep wounds to mind. It is the very ambiguity of these texts that mark them as political works, meant to reconcile the divided Florence rather than support one faction over the other, it is in his theological works, such as the *Contra Falsos Ecclesie Professores* in which he espouses a "*reductio ad unum* of all men to the pope."[55]

---

[54] ad primam siquidem legem pertinent duo prima precepta iustitie; positiva autem est duplex, scilicet divina et humana et sic est duplex iustitia. Divina autem est duplex, scilicet vetus et nova. Humana autem est duplex, scilicet civilis et ecclesiastica. Civilis autem est duplex, scilicet imperialis et municipalis.

[55] Davis (1960), 672.

The De Bono Communi

Introduction to the *De Bono Communi*[56]

Remigius dei Girolami is by no means the first author to discuss the *bonum communi*.[57] This idea has a long history of development in the Middle Ages, and he is building on this tradition. Girolami is especially beholden to the discussion of the law in relation to the *bonum communi* in *Quaestio* 90 of Thomas Aquinas' Summa Theologica: "Consequently, since the law is chiefly ordained to the common good, any other precept in regard to some individual work, must need be devoid of the nature of a law, save in so far as it regards the common good. Therefore, every law is ordained to the common good."[58]

Thomas Aquinas also discusses the nature of this *bonum communi*, however, which he identifies as happiness.[59] What makes up the common good, the *bonum communi*? This question provides a natural topic of discussion in Remigius dei Girolami's *De Bono Communi*. Yet, he never once discusses what precisely this good is. Instead, the focus of this text is in setting out the argument that the *bonum communi* is more to be loved than the good of the individual: "the common good is, without doubt, to be preferred over the good of the individual and

---

[56] The Latin text I used for this translation is from the edition in Panella (2014), 146-221. This edition also contains copious notes and a translation into Italian.

[57] Cf. for example in Kempshall (1999) and Keys (2006). For a very in-depth discussion of the *De Bono Communi* and the *De Bono Pacis* and an extensive commentary on both see Panella (2014).

58 Translated by Fathers of the English Dominican Province. Unde oportet quod, cum lex maxime dicatur secundum ordinem ad bonum commune, quodcumque aliud praeceptum de particulari opere non habeat rationem legis nisi secundum ordinem ad bonum commune. Et ideo omnis lex ad bonum commune ordinatur.

[59] Thomas Aquinas *Summa Theologica* 90.

the good of the many over the good of one single person. This can be proven with a variety of arguments."[60]

This text arises as a response to the abandonment of regard for the common good. In discussing this, Remigius quotes II *Timothy* 3, the puffed up and proud individuals foreseen by Saint Paul find their home in the Italy of Girolami, this allusion to the ongoing conflict between the Black and White Guelfs, as well as, conflicts between other factions in the city:

> ...who, because of their very great and inordinate love for themselves have neglected the good of their communities, because they have little or no care for them and driven on by a demonic spirit, have thrown the castles, cities, provinces and the entire region into confusion through strife and destroyed them by assault.[61]

The purpose of this text, rather than supporting one faction over the other, is to convince these various factions to put the common good of the city over their own, ending the cycles of violence and bringing peace. The argument of the text can be broken up into three main sections. In the first section, Remigius gives various theological, philosophical, historical, and natural examples of the love for the *bonum communi* surpassing that of the individual good. In the second section, he discusses the *bonum communi* in the context of the relationship of the

---

[60] I. bonum comune indubitanter preferendum est bono particulari et bonum multitudinis bono unius singularis persone. Quod quidem multipliciter declarari potest.

[61] I. qui quidem, propter nimium amorem atque inordinatum sui ipsorum bona comunia negligentes, parum vel nichil de ipsis curando, spiritu diabolico agitati, castra civitates provincias totamque regionem hostilitatibus inordinatis confundunt et destruunt incessanter.

part to the whole. In the final section, Remigius adopts the format of objections to his premise with responses to these objections used in the *Summa Theologica* of Thomas Aquinas.

Sections 1 through 8:

The first eight sections of the *De Bono Communi* are dedicated to providing examples for holding the *bonum communi* as more important the private good. The whole argument begins in sections one and two with a microcosm of the whole argument applying examples from Scripture and the saints in section one, and of pagan philosophers in section two. Running from section three to section eight Girolami presents a progression of examples that rise from creatures with "natural love," in this case water, through animals, pagan examples, examples from the Old and New Testaments and the saints. This progression, rising through the "ordinem caritatis" seems to mirror the Neo-Platonic progression toward the good or the beautiful.[62]

This structure allows Remigius to present this text as it could have been used as source material for sermons,[63] with arguments on two levels. Firstly, arguments that increase in validity, the animal more valid than that which has only natural love, human examples, even pagan, more valid than that with animal love, the Scriptural

---

[62] Cf. for example Plotinus Ennead 1.6 and the discussion of the progression towards the beautiful. For more on the Neo Platonic influence on Thomas Auqinas see Hankey (2011). Remigius dei Girolami too shows his reliance on Neoplatonism, especially in his reliance on Dionysius the Areopagite.

[63] The Sermones de Pace, for example, refer to the *De Bono Communi* and the *De Bono Pacis* five times.

examples more valid than pagan. Secondly, the progression is also a temporal progression, moving forward from the Old Testament to the New Testament to the Saints. Both progressions work in tandem to underscore the importance of the *bonum communi.*

Section I: Quod quidem multipliciter declarari potest. Et primo multiplici auctoritate sacre scripture tam canonis utriusque testamenti quam etiam sanctorum.[64]

Following the setup of the issue that necessitates the writing of this text, Remigius delves immediately into examples that show that the bonum communi is to be loved more than the *bonum particulari,* of the private individual. The use of Scriptural proofs and examples is a common one in the works of Remigius. Their use is more prominent in the *Nine Sermons on Peace* and in the *De Iustitia.* In this first section, Remigius combines anecdotes of persons putting the *bonum communi* first with quotations from Scripture that support this position. Especially interesting are the choices of Onias and Caiaphas in this section, since this would be one of the first parts of the text seen by a reader. This choice plays into the moderation of justice Remigius discusses in the *De Iustitia,* in which, the dispenser of justice must always be cognizant of whether or not carrying out justice is in the interest of the *bonum communi.* In these cases, despite acting unjustly, Onias and Caiaphas were acting for the welfare of the people of the whole:

---

[64] "This can be proven with a variety of argument. First: many in the authority of sacred Scripture, whether in the canon of the Old or New Tetaments or even in the saints.

a. The first example is from *Maccabees* 4:4-6, in which Onias, who hands over his own kinsman to the king in order to bring peace.

b. The second example consists of two similar quotations *Ecclesiastes* 4:28 and *Isaiah* 32:17, both of which discuss the *bonum communi* in terms of peace.

c. The third is another anecdote, from *John* 11:50, of Caiaphas, who, like Onias, is willing to sacrifice one person, that is, Christ, for the welfare of many.

d. The fourth is another set of quotation, this time from I *Corinthians* 13:5 and from Augustine's *Regula*, which discuss how love leads a person to put the *bonum communi* over their own.

e. The final example is another quotation, from Boethius, which again discusses how a good is better if it is in common.

Section II: probatur auctoritate infidelium.[65]

The philosophy, mythology and history of Classical antiquity hold a central place in the philosophical tradition of the Middle Ages. Paul the Deacon, John of Salisbury, Godfrey of Fontaines,[66] among many other notable Medieval scholars use Classical sources.[67] Dante Alighieri, a contemporary and possible student of Remigius,[68] famously places various figures from antiquity, Vergil, Cassius, Brutus etc. at various levels of his Inferno. Petrarch goes so far as to say: "what is history, but the praise of

---

[65] "proven by pagan authorities."

[66] Cf. Mäkinen (2011), 131.

[67] Cf. Davis (1974). See also Smalley (1971), 165-194.

[68] Ottman (2004), 233. Cf. also Davis (1959), who is doubtful of the student teacher relationship, but admits it may be possible.

Rome?"[69] The vast majority of references Remigius makes, to sources of Classical antiquity, are to the works of Aristotle, for which he is beholden again to Thomas Aquinas, whose use of Aristotle in the *Summa Theologica* and whose *Commentaries on Aristotle* pave the way for more extensive use in the Medieval West. To give an idea of the importance played by Classical authors in Remigius dei Girolami, Aristotle, whom Remigius dei Girolami refers to as "the philosopher," is quoted as often in the *De Bono Communi* as Scripture is. The various texts referred to in this section all focus not only on the fact that a good is better if it is in common than if it is an individual good, but that this has the consequence that an individual member of the community ought to defend the community and even lay down his life for it.

a. The first quotations come from the *Ethics* of Aristotle. This quotation is used by Remigius to set up a hierarchy of communities, each one more to be loved than the one before because they are larger wholes:

> This is as if he said that however much good is in common so much more is it to be loved, that is, the good of a city is more than the good of a private citizen and the good of a province, which contains many cities, more than the good of one city. From whence also and as a consequence the good of a kingdom is more to be loved than the good of a province and the good of the universal church more than the good of one kingdom.[70]

---

[69] Davis (1974), 30.

[70] II. Quanto bonum est comunius tanto est magis amandum, scilicet bonum civitatis magis quam bonum unius civis et bonum provincie que

This is one of the few times in the *De Bono Communi* in which Remigius breaks out of the discussion of the relationship of the individual person with the community they belong to directly. Interesting is that his support for the papacy, which comes out in other texts, such as the *contra falsos ecclesie doctores*, can be seen here, in the remark that the church is more to be loved than an individual kingdom, a point of view that he generally avoids displaying in this text. Here he allows it to come through as part of the progression of communities, since the universal church includes a number of different kingdoms within it.

  b. Following the Aristotelian quotations, are four from Cicero: from the *Oratione pro Quinto Ligurio ad Iulium Caesarem;* from the *De Officiis;* from the *Invectia contra Salustium* and another from the *De Officiis.*

  c. Finally, is a short quotation attributed to Cato: pugna pro patria. A quotation used often in medieval philosophy.[71]

Section III: probatur exemplis in creaturis habentibus solum amorem naturalem.[72]

Beginning the ascent toward the weightier examples from Scripture are creatures that have only "natural love." Remigius discusses these "creatures:" which are water, air, earth, and fire acting against their own natures to fulfill the higher law of the "nature of the whole universe," that

---

multas continet civitates magis quam bonum unius civitatis. Unde et per consequens bonum regni magis amandum est quam bonum unius provincie et bonum universalis ecclesie magis quam bonum unius regni.

[71] Post (1964), 441-442.

[72] Proven by examples concerning creatures that have only natural love."

no vacuum should exist. Even these creatures, which have no rationality, put the good of the larger community, the universe as a whole, over their own personal good, their own natures. Remigius gives four examples of this:

a. The first example is of water moving upward into a phial contrary to its nature when the air in the phial is consumed by a candle.

b. The second example is of air descending, contrary to its nature, into a vase filled with a liquid as the liquid escapes the bottom of the vase.

c. The third example is from book four of Aristotle's *Physics* chapters 6-9, in which Aristotle discusses the functioning of a *clepsydra*, a water clock.

d. The fourth example is from Augustine, the second book of *de Origine Anime*, in which he explains that two bodies, air, and water, cannot occupy the same space at once. If then, air is not allowed to escape from a vessel being submerged in water, no water will enter. If the air can escape, the water will ascend into the vessel.

e. Finally, Remigius mentions that fire and earth act in the same way, going contrary to their nature if required by greater universal laws.

Section IV: probatur exemplis creaturarum habentium amorem animalem.[73]

The majority of this section is a quotation from the *Exameron* of Ambrose of Milan.[74] Specifically, the section in which he discusses the habits and lifestyles of bees. Interestingly, the bee is the only creature that has "animate

---

[73] "Proven by examples of creatures that have animate love."

[74] Ambrose *Exameron* V, 21 70.

love," that is presented by Remigius, although the *Exameron* does discuss other creatures that hold their community above themselves, like cranes for example.[75] The nature of the bee, as presented by Ambrose, fits very well into the paradigm Remigius is attempting to lay out for the proper relationship a citizen should have with their community. The bee holds all things in common and works solely for the improvement and furthering of the community. They also naturally love their king and put the life of their king over their own. The quotation from the *Exameron*, which summarizes the discussion of bees in Aristotle,[76] assumes understanding of the nature of the community on the part of the bees, allowing them to be an example for the humans in Florence, where the discussion of bees in Thomas Aquinas gives them a "certain social tendency," but denies them a community on the scale of humanity.[77]

Not only does this example from the Exameron underscore the importance of the community, furthering Remigius' argumentation, it also connects Remigius' discussion to the works of antiquity. Not only those of Aristotle but the discussion of bees in Vergil's *Georgics* as well.[78] This sets up the next section of his examples, in which he discusses notable figures from Roman antiquity that held the *bonum communi* over their own.

---

[75] Ibid.
[76] Steel (1999), 280.
[77] Thomas Aquinas *Commentary on the Politics* I.1 36.
[78] Vergil *Georgics* IV 149-227.

Section V: probatur exemplis creaturarum habentium amorem rationalem idest hominum infidelium.[79]

The examples given in this section make up the most extensive individual section in this part of the text, reflect the importance given to Remigius in the classical world. The examples fall into two broad categories: 1. examples of Romans who lay down their lives for the good of their state and 2. Examples of Romans who, while in a position of power, do not enrich themselves at the expense of the state, therefore, putting the good of the community above their own. These two categories mirror the two aspects of the creatures with "animate love," from the previous section, who put their lives on the line and put the community good above their own.

One interesting aspect of these examples from Classical history is that most are from the Roman Republic, rather than examples from the time of the kings or the empire.[80] This not only utilizes examples that resonate with the citizens of Republican Florence but also allows Remigius to create a solution for political crisis focused on the individual citizen, without reliance on a king or emperor.[81]

  a. The opening of this section deals with how the various organs of the body work to put the good of the whole body above the good of themselves. For example, the arms cover the head to defend it from blows.

---

[79] "proven by examples of creatures that have rational love, that is by pagan examples."

[80] Non-Roman examples of virtue are cancelled out by non-Roman examples of vice.

[81] Newman (2016), 13.

b. The first example is of Lucius Valerius, who despite his consulship, died a poor man and needed to be provided a funeral at public expense.

c. Quintus Cincinattus is the next example. He was elected dictator and, when the crisis was averted, returned to his farm labor.

d. Fabricius, who refused to accept a bribe from Pyrrhus, and refused to take an opportunity to have Pyrrhus murdered.

e. Marcus Curtius threw himself, fully armed, into a gaping chasm that had opened in the middle of the city, as this was prophesied to be the only way to close it up.

f. King Zaleucus, who showed both mercy and justice, took one of his own eyes, as well as, one of his son's, who was convicted of adultery and should have been blinded according to the law.

g. Torquatus, who executed his own son for disobeying his commands in battle.

h. Marcus Regulus, who was captured by the Carthaginians, was sent to Rome as an envoy to convince the Senate to come to terms with the Carthaginians. Rather than doing so, he spoke against peace, since it was against the interest of the Roman people. When he returned to Carthage, as he had sworn to do, he was put to death.

i. Codrus, the king of Athens, dressed as a common soldier in battle, due to the fact, there was a prophecy that if Codrus died Athens would not fall.

j. Anaximenes of Lamsacus tricked Alexander the Great into sparing the city.

k. Cato the Younger, who killed himself, rather than seeing the Republic ruled by Julius Caesar.

Section VI: probatur in fidelibus veteris testamenti.[82]

Remigius uses only three examples from the Old Testament. In each example, the figure in question exposes themselves to the risk of death for the good of the people.

a. The first example is Moses, who offers himself to God in expiation for the sins of the Jewish nation. Because of this God only punishes twenty thousand (or three thousand) with death, instead of destroying the entirety of the people.

b. The second example is of King David, who risks death when confronting an unarmed giant in order to save the people of Israel. Later, he also offers himself as a substitute for the nation of Israel for punishment.

c. Finally, Remigius discusses the person of Judas Maccabeus, who fights overwhelming odds and dies in battle to free Israel from invaders.

Section VII: probatur in fidelibus novi testamenti quantum ad canonem.[83]

The shortest section in this part of the text is dealing with examples from the New Testament, in which, Remigius contents himself with two examples: St. Paul and Christ.

a. In using St. Paul as an example, Remigius discusses three passages from the *Epistles: 1st Corinthians* 10, *2nd Corinthians* 13 and *Romans* 9. These quota-

---

[82] "Proven by the Faithful of the Old Testament."
[83] "Proven by the Faithful of the Canonical New Testament."

tions once again lay out the same two categories of putting the *bonum communi* above one's own interest: 1. in *1st Corinthians* and *2nd Corinthians*, St. Paul discusses seeking what is useful for the community as a whole, rather than what is useful for him. He, like Valerius and Cincinattus, is not interested in his own wealth, but the proper stewardship of the community as a whole. 2. In *Romans* 9, putting one's life on the line for the community is discussed. In this case St. Paul is even willing to lose his salvation for the sake of the community.

b.   The discussion of Christ in this context also hinges on a quotation from the *Epistles*. In this case from *Hebrews* 13, as well as, in *Matthew* 20. In this example Remigius focuses on the willingness of Christ to sacrifice himself for the good of humanity.

Section VIII: probatur in fidelibus novi testamenti extra canonem.[84]

The final section consists of four "exempla de aliis sanctis extra canonem."[85] These saints, imitating Christ, are willing to put their lives on the line for the common good, and two of the examples provide this sacrifice. The four examples are chosen to represent the ranks of the church, a pope, an archbishop, and a bishop, but also of the state. The final example is of a king, as we saw in the section on pagan examples. There is a distinct de-emphasis on the king, and he is merely called a "laico," a layperson, in the introduction to the section.

---

[84] "Proven by the Faithful of the New Tesament outside the Canon."
[85] "Examples of other saints from outside the Canon."

a. The first example is Pope Leo I. In order to save the city of Rome, he put his own life at risk by appealing directly to Attila, whom he begs to spare the city of Rome. In revealing the reason that Attila acquiesces to Leo I, Remigius is able to turn this one example into a double example. He tells those who mock him for not attacking: "I provided for myself and for you. For I saw standing on his right hand a most puissant warrior with bared sword threatening me and saying: 'If you do not obey him, you will be destroyed with all your host.'"[86] Attila then bears to be mocked and questioned to save his community, putting their good above his own

b. The second example is Archbishop Thomas Becket, who was: "ready to die for God and for the defense of justice and for the liberty of the church."[87] While the church is the highest community in the works of Remigius, he also immediately hands himself over to those seeking to kill him, to keep the other clerics at Canterbury from coming to harm. Moreover, important here is the idea of justice. A virtue explored in the *De Iustitia* and one without which a community cannot function.

c. The example of Lupus of Trecassinus appears an odd one, as he seems to contradict the idea of sacrificing oneself for the good of the community. He opens the gates of his city to the army of Attila,

---

[86] Providi michi et vobis. Vidi enim in dextris eius fortissimum militem evaginato gladio stantem michique minantem et dicentem 'Nisi huic parueris, cum tuis omnibus interibis.'

[87] pro Deo mori paratus et pro defensione iustitie et pro ecclesie libertate.

which would seem to be destructive to the community, rather than a saving effort. This saint, however, plays into a previous statement made by Remigius, that: "God gives virtue and protection to those who expose themselves to peril for the good of the many."[88] By opening the gates and trusting in God, Lupus exposes himself to danger and is protected by God. God then confounds the invaders, who leave without even seeing the defenders.

d. The final example is of King Ludovicus of the Franks, who dies on Crusade. This example forms a couplet with the first in this section, a pope and an emperor, the rallying points for the factions of the Investiture conflict and the Guelfs and Ghibbellines. This seems a delicate prospect, to attempt to heal division in the community using examples dealing with the causes of the division. Remigius gets around this by having the very cause of the conflict put the good of the opposing faction over their own good, pope Leo I meets with Attila, not to attempt to convert him, not even to ask him to spare the churches or the clergy, but specifically to turn him away from the city of Rome. King Ludovicus dies on Crusade "for the defense of the Holy Land and the Christian people."[89] Not for the good of his own kingdom, but for that of the entirety of Christendom. If the focus of division can put aside their personal good, or that of

---

[88] Deus dat virtutem et presidium exponentibus se periculis pro bono multitudinis.

[89] pro defensione Terre sancte et populi christiani.

their faction, and put the *bonum communi* first, then how much more should the citizen of Florence do the same

Sections 9 through 17: The Part and the Whole

The next broad discussion, comprising of sections 9-17, of the *De Bono Communi* establishes the reason that a citizen should put the *bonum communi* over their own good. The premise of this discussion hinges on the idea that the entirety of the city or community forms one whole, of which each citizen is a part. In this understanding, Remigius is especially beholden to the Aristotelian description of the relationship of *polis* and citizen as an organism within its constituent organs. Such as, the hand in relationship to the whole body.[90] While there are certainly questions as to whether Aristotle's description merits understanding as "implicit totalitarianism,"[91] and some scholars have come to doubt this interpretation of this text as putting the community and its citizens in the same context as a living organism and its organs,[92] Remigius is very beholden to this description. Remigius adopts the imagery of the hand in relationship to the body in his own discussion in section 9. It is in the understanding of the community as a whole, of which each person is a part, which allows for the generalized nature of the political discussion in the *De Bono Communi*. Since this does not predicate the victory of one faction over the other, but instead rests on the idea that the part, the citi-

---

[90] Aristotle *Politics* 1253a18-29.
[91] Barnes (1990), 263.
[92] Mayhew (1997), 325-340.

zen should love the whole more than himself, because it is more beautiful, and more noble.

Because the basic premise of this section is that the individual is to love the common good, the good of the community, more than his own, Remigius examines this idea from the various aspects of love: what is loved, what loves, the various causes of love, the effects of love and the signs of love. Remigius shows that in every case the whole is more to be loved than the part.

Section IX: Idem probatur ratione sumpta ex parte obiecti sive ab omnibus naturaliter amatorum. [93]

Remigius dei Girolami begins his argumentation that the part should love the whole more than itself by discussing those things which are naturally loved by all. These things are: the common good; beauty; existence; God and happiness. In this section, he describes how these naturally loved aspects apply more to the community and the whole, than to the individual and the part. Therefore, the part is lead to love the whole more than itself.

a. The first thing that is loved by all is the common good. This pertains more to the whole than the part because part is included in the whole, but not vice versa.

b. The second is beauty. Remigius argues that the beauty of a part is dependent on the whole that it is a part of. This is true both of things which are usually considered beautiful, which can be ugly in context: "a flower is beautiful in the meadow, not in the dung or manure pile." That which is ugly on its own may also seem

---

[93] "The same is proven by arguments made with respect to the object; that is, to those things which are loved naturally by all."

beautiful in the context of the whole: "the colors black and ashen, although they are ugly in and of themselves, are beautiful as a part of the whole painting."

c. A lengthy section is devoted to discussing the existence of the part being dependent on the existence of the whole. Here, Remigius employs the Aristotelian image of the individual being a part of a community, like an organ is part of the body, specifically the hand. He likens a hand cut off from the body, as one that is analogous to a hand in a painting, or on a statue. That is not a hand in actuality, but is called one anyway. He broadens this image to include the citizens of Florence who is "stone or painted," because they too, while called a citizen, cannot be one in actuality. Here Remigius also discusses the city of Florence by name. Which is an unusual occurrence in the text, creting a play on words, the Florentine becomes a Flerentine, a weeper, due to the destruction of the state.

d. God also says, Remigius, has more in common with the whole than with the part, because "God is striven for by all in a community...since all things are communally in Him...also since He is Himself communally in all creatures." In consequence, Remigius says that the love of Gods necessitates the love of the community as well.

e. The final thing that is naturally loved by all, is happiness. Happiness is described by Remigius as being something that is naturally shared: "perfect happiness is not possible in only one human, but is pushed outward." Not only does this lead the part to love the whole on account of happiness, but the fact that if the whole, the community, is destroyed, then happiness is impossible because it: "cannot exist when nature is found to be deficient." As an example of this, Remigius discusses Ovid, for whom it was impossible to be happy when deprived of his homeland.

Section X: Idem probatur ex parte subiecti sive hominum amantium.[94]

The second, rather short, section in this series discusses who loves, i.e. humans, and how humans naturally love the whole more than themselves. The driving point is that humans naturally love those in a closer relationship to themselves, more than those who are further removed: "...kinsmen more than strangers and among kinsmen he loves his son more than his brothers..." Humans, ought to, love the common good more than themselves, because they are a part of the whole. In addition, the part stands in a closer relationship to the whole than to itself. The part is closer to the whole than it is to itself, because the whole is both the origin of its existence as well as the preservation of its existence. Because without the whole the part does not exist. If the part cannot exist outside the whole, then it cannot form any relationships on its own accord. Remigius says that: "joining presupposes existence," and is therefore, in a closer relationship with the whole than it is with anything else.

---

[94] "The same is proven with respect to the subject, that is, with respect to humans who love."

Section XI: Idem probatur ex parte causarum ipsius amoris quantum ad causam sine qua non.[95]

Section eleven begins a series of five sections that form a subcategory dealing with the causes of love. The first of these is the most important, cause without which love cannot exist. This reason *sine qua non* is a relationship, knowledge of that which is loved: "intensity of love naturally follows from the intensity of knowledge." In the rest of the section, Remigius discusses the ways in which the whole is better known to the part, than the part is to itself. This necessitates that the part loves the whole more than it loves itself.

a. The part knows the whole "before it knows itself." Because the whole is known to the part before it knows itself, it knows it better and therefore, loves it more.

b. The second and third points Remigius makes seem to be in contradiction to each other. The second point he makes is that the part is more easily able to comprehend a "part" than a whole because: "it is easier for something to be known imperfectly than perfectly and diminished rather than according to the whole." This is because of a: "fault of our soul, which naturally flees from this type of difficulty, seeking quiet more than work." Nevertheless, since it is easier to comprehend something imperfectly, a whole is comprehended as a confusion, rather than as a union of its parts. This is laid out in the third point, that it is easier to comprehend a crowd than the individuals within it, and a sum of

---

[95] "The same is proven with respect to the cause of his love, that cause without which it does not exist."

money than the individual coins. Through this method of comprehension, the whole is better known to the part than the "part" is.

Section XII: Idem probatur ex parte causarum moventium, et primo ex parte virtutis.[96]

What moves one person to love another? Following the discussion of relationship, Remigius moves on to discussing how virtue instills mutual love, and how the virtue of the whole instills a greater love for the whole in the part, than the part has for itself.

a. Remigius spends the first two paragraphs of this section discussing how virtue leads to mutual love. It is the recognition of intellectual and moral virtues, which exist within each person. That leads humans to love one another, even if they are unknown to one another. Here Remigius discusses the friendship of Augustine and Hieronymus, who never met, but loved one another nonetheless.

b. It is because of the natural love for virtue which creates friendship, that the part loves the whole more than itself. Because there is more virtue in the whole than in the part: "the citizen can be made more virtuous in every way...in conjunction with the state than existing on his own."

c. The remainder of this section is dedicated to a discussion of how the virtue of the part can be increased by its participation in the whole. For example, a student is able to become more learned through his interaction with other students and learned men in the city,

---

[96] "The same is proven with respect to the cause of motion, especially with respect to virtue."

where he would not be able to increase on his own. Morally too, the citizen is spurred on to greater virtue by the example and support of his fellow citizens: "since he is more spurred on to virtue and good works by the examples of other virtuous men."

Section XIII: Idem probatur ex parte corporalis delectabilitatis.[97]

In this section, Remigius discusses a cause of love that is "especially prevelant in the youth." This is a physical attraction. Human senses are naturally attuned to beauty, and so the more beautiful something is, the more it is loved. It is this natural love that humans have for the beautiful that leads them to love their city, more than themselves.

a. After establishing the natural desire for beauty that leads humans to love the beautiful, Remigius discusses why this desire for beauty leads the part to love the whole, the citizen to love the city. "First...that which is more beautiful is more loved." Like virtue, the city contains more beauty than the individual citizen does, because there can be many beautiful people who inhabit it: "The beauty of an entire field in bloom is greater than that of one individual flower." The individual parts, then contribute to the greater beauty of the whole, and therefore love the greater beauty of the whole than they love themselves. Conversely, the whole gives beauty to the individual parts, as it gives the part existence. Therefore, it is loved more as the

---

[97] "The same is proven with respect to bodily enjoyment."

cause of beauty than the part, which receives its beauty from it.

b. In the final paragraphs of this section, Remigius discusses the consequences that this love has for the citizens of Florence because the destruction of the city makes it impossible for the part to have "pleasantness." In this section, Remigius also uses the name of Florence to create a play on words illustrating the plight of the city, as he did in section nine. Here he plays on the sound of "Firenze," as the common people of the city pronounce "Fiorenza," comparing it to the sound of disgust made by the French: "fi fi."

Section XIV: Idem probatur ex parte temporalis utilitatis.[98]

Section fourteen is created as a couplet to section thirteen. While physical attraction is what creates love in the young, it is usefulness that causes love in the old. The usefulness of someone or something causes love because of: "imperfect or … defective nature. For all men are naturally defective." Because each individual is unable to do everything themselves, they love those who are able to do those things which they themselves lack.

a. Remigius spends the next three paragraphs giving examples to support this argument. First, are pagans who love those they should despise on account of their usefulness. He gives the example of the emperor Tiberius, who: "loved Jesus, desiring to be cured of leprosy by Him." The same holds true for Christians, who love non-Christians: "Saracens and Jews" and cit-

---

[98] "The same is proven with respect to temporal utility."

ies who love other cities because of mutual aid. To underscore his point, Remigius also points out that the natural tendency for humans to live in a community: "that one may supplement where another is lacking since one makes shoes, another houses, another clothing, another plows the ground, another makes arms" is a prime example of this type of love.

b. Like section nine and thirteen, Remigius closes his discussion with a direct reference to the city of Florence. He asks how the citizens of Florence can find any use in the city or in one another since the city is in a state of destruction. He also echoes the closing of section thirteen by again playing on the pronunciation of "Firenze" and the connotation of a bad smell.

Section XV: Idem probatur ex parte similitudinis.[99]

In the final section that Remigius uses to discuss the causes of love, he looks back at section ten, which discusses the subject of love, which is humans: "Every man naturally loves those who are more closely related to him." In section fifteen, he discusses similarity as a cause of love: "since, then, every creature natrually loves itself, it natrually loves everything in which that same entity is discovered."

a. Remigius first discusses what is meant by similarity in a broad sense. For example, similarity in position: "the love by which a weighty object, existing in its own place, loves another living in a similar place is greater than the love by which it would love one existing in a different place." Important as well, is the distinction

---

[99] "The same is proven with respect to similarity."

between actuality and potentiality. As things with actual being are more similar to one another, and therefore have greater love for one another.

b. Remigius then goes through a hierarchy of similarities and discusses which of these creates the greatest love: "therefore a human loves the animate, such as a tree, more than the inanimate, such as a rock..."

c. The last part of this section, is the discussion of how the similarity of the part to the whole, leads the part to love the whole more than itself. Since the part has no existence outside of the part, and since the whole has "existence in actuality," the part is more similar to the whole than it is to itself. Therefore, it loves the whole more than itself.

Section XVI: Idem probatur ratione sumpta ex parte effectuum amoris.[100]

In section sixteen, Remigius breaks with the discussion of the causes of love, which have occupied the text over the last few sections and moves to a discussion of the effects of love. This switch in the topic, however, would lead the reader to expect another series of sections dealing with it; instead, the entire topic is contained within one section, perhaps to underscore that the causes of love bring the part to love the whole more than itself or the signs in the following section. Remigius discusses five effects of love in this section: 1. the unification of the lover with the beloved; 2. mutual indwelling; 3. ecstasy; 4. zeal and 5. the preservation of the lover.

---

[100] "The same is proven by arguments made in respect to the effect of love."

a. Love unites the lover with the beloved: "either formally according to the affect, since love is in a certain sense a union, or effectively according to fact, just as marrying joins formally...through which it is possible without corruption to become one from two, since they speak together, share together, abide together and suchlike." Since the whole has actual being the union of the part to the whole is "a union of an entity in actuality" while the part, which does not have "actual being" cannot have this type of a union with itself, and therefore loves the whole more than itself.

b. The second point, mutual indwelling, is similar to the first in definition: "like the unity of the lover to the beloved, mutual indwelling focuses on the close association of the lovers to one another". In this case, however, the closeness is mutual. The consequence for the relationship between the part and the whole also mirrors that of the first point: "for this reason the part loves the whole more than itself, since certainly the part is in the whole and vice versa...the part, however, is not individual in itself."

c. The third effect, ecstasy, allows Remigius to distinguish between a proper love, which participates in divine love, and improper criminal love, which: "is no true love." Ecstasy, which "puts a human outside of himself," ennobles the lover and moves them toward the "superior nature" and therefore seeks the good. For example, loves the community more than himself.

d. Fourth is zeal. Remigius writes this as çelus, which could be interpreted either as zealous or jealous.

While either translation could be used for much of the discussion, the description of this effect: "someone is said to be zealous...when he attempts to keep away, as much as he is able to, that which goes against the good of his friend, the integrity of his faith and the will and honor of God," fits the sense of zeal more than that of jealousy. This understanding of zeal, the defense of what is loved, is also what shows that the part loves the whole more than itself. For example, the citizen keeps the city safe more eagerly than himself, and his own good and safety depends on that of the city.

e. The same reasoning that the safety of the individual is dependent on the safety of the community is what drives the final effect of love: the preservation of the lover. Since an individual's natural love for themselves leads them to seek their own preservation, they love the city more than themselves, due to, the fact that preservation of the part comes from the whole.

Section XVII: Idem probatur ratione sumpta ex parte signorum amoris.[101]

The final section in this series, before Remigius transitions to discussing and responding to the possible objections to the text, deals with the signs of love, of which Remigius discusses four: 1. examination; 2. obedience; 3. the tolerance for work and 4. distribution of material goods.

---

[101] "The same is proven by arguments made in respect to the signs of love."

a. For the first half of this section, Remigius discusses these four signs of love, and how they show that the part loves the whole more than itself, generally for the same reasons that he has discussed all along. Obedience, for example is owed to the state because it is "wiser...understand the truth more clearly." In distributing material goods, Remigius even returns to the metaphor of the citizen of the city being an organ of the body, and it would be remiss for the hand not to pass on food to the rest of the body.

b. Remigius ends this discussion unusually. This is the only place outside of the sections in which he discusses the possible objections to his argument that he presents a *caveat*: "these things are said to be signs, not proofs." The signs of love only present a potentiality that love exists, and Remigius gives several examples of someone exhibiting a sign of love for someone, despite their actual hatred for that person: "occasionally someone obeys him whom he hates from fear or so that he may secretly cause him injury."

Sections 18 through 21: Objections to this Premise and their Solutions

The *De Bono Communi* closes with four sections in which Remigius lays out and solves issues with his premise and argumentation. These issues are presented in the form of objections, each of which receives a response resolving and correcting the counterargument. In Section XVIII deals with problems of the examples given, Section IX with the object of love, Section XX with the subject of love and Section XXI the causes of love.

This method of establishing and dealing with objections to the premises established by Remigius is adapted from a similar method used by Thomas Aquinas in the *Summa Theologica*. Unlike in the Summa, however, Remigius has grouped all of the objections into these last four sections, Thomas Aquinas begins each of the parts of his *Summa* with the objections and their solutions, before then beginning the actual argumentation. This style of exposition is inherited by Thomas Aquinas and Remigius from Averroes,[102] whose interest in Aristotle was also instrumental in the development of Thomas Aquinas' philosophy.

---

[102] Abu al-Walid Muhammad ibn Ahmad ibn Rushd, a twelfth century Muslim theologian and philosopher.

The De Bono Communi

by Brother Remigius O.P. of Florence

1. That the Common Good Should be Preferred to the Good of One's Own Private Affairs is Proven by Many Authorities in the Sacred Scripture.

The prophecy of the apostle Paul in second *Timothy* says that: "there follows close a perilous time, and there will be those who love themselves, who are greedy, puffed up and proud etc..." [103] this is seen clearly fulfilled in these times and in modern men (alas, most of all in us Italians); who, because of their very great and inordinate love for themselves have neglected the good of their communities, because they have little or no care for them. These men, driven on by a demonic spirit, have thrown the castles,

---

[103] II *Timothy* 3: 1-2.

cities, provinces and the entire region into confusion through strife and destroyed them by assault. According to the order of love, of which is written in the *Song of Songs*: "he set love in me,"[104] the common good is without doubt to be preferred over the good of the individual and the good of the many over the good of one single person. This can be proven with a variety of arguments.

First of all, by many in the authority of Sacred Scripture, whether in the canon of the Old or New Testaments or even in the saints.

Of Onias, the high priest and perfect man, is written in second *Maccabees* that: "he went to the king not as an accuser of the citizenry, but for the good of the community, considering the whole multitude in his own mind, for he saw that, without the providence of the king, it would be impossible to bring peace to the state and to hold back Simon from his folly."[105] From this it is apparent that for peace, which is without doubt good for the community just as health of body is certainly for the good of the community of the entire person, he even submitted himself to the king and procured, through the misfortune of one troubled kinsman, the good of the community for all men, compelling him to the order of love from which he had strayed. Of this Onias is again written, at the conclusion of second *Macabbees*, that he was: "a good and kindhearted man, modest of look, mild of manner, proper in speaking and schooled in virtues from childhood."[106]

---

[104] *Song of Songs* 2:4.
[105] II *Maccabees* 4: 4-6.
[106] II *Macabbees* 15:12

The same is said in *Ecclesiastes*: "contend even unto death for justice,"[107] through which, you may be sure, the good of the community for the many, which is peace, is acquired and maintained. In agreement with this is *Isaiah*: "The work of justice will be peace."[108]

The same says Caiaphas, who was certainly a wicked man, but being compelled by the uncreated spirit of truth toward love, in *John*: "It is better for you that one man should die for the people than that the entire nation should perish."[109]

The same is said in first *Corinthians*: "love does not search out those things that belong to it;"[110] blessed Augustine expounding on this in the *Rules* says that this is to be understood in such a way because: "love puts the community interests before its own,"[111] and again later: "however much more you care about the common good than about your own, so much more will you learn to advance."

Boethius makes the same point when he says: "Every good brought forth into the community shines more beautifully for all."[112]

This suffices, for the present, for this first point.

2. The Same Proven by Pagan Authorities

The Philosopher says in the first book of the *Ethics*: "though, indeed, good is the same both for an individual

---

[107] *Ecclesiastes* 4:28

[108] *Isaiah* 32:17

[109] *John* 11:50

[110] I *Corinthians* 13:5

[111] Augustine *Regula* Caput V: 31

[112] Cf. Dante Alighieri *The Purgatory of Dante Alighieri*. Butler, Arthur J. (ed. and trans.). (London: MacMillan and Co., 1880), pg. 178.

and for a community, it is better and more perfect to support and save a community; it is certainly pleasant for one person, but truly more divine for whole peoples and nations"[113] i.e., for the many. This is as if he said that however much good is in common so much more is it to be loved, that is, the good of a city is more than the good of a private citizen and the good of a province, which contains many cities, more than the good of one city. From whence also and as a consequence the good of a kingdom is more to be loved than the good of a province and the good of the universal church more than the good of one kingdom.

In the ninth chapter too he says: "truly then – to whit: it is – of the devoted man – that is, said – that he distributes much for the love of his friends and would die for his country if it would be necessary."[114] In chapter one, too, he says that the most principle virtue and the greatest art and architect is the community.[115] In chapter eight of the *Topics* too he says: "a perverse associate is he who hinders the work of the community."[116]

Similarly, Tullius says in the *Oration in Defense of Quintus Ligarius*: "fortune has anything better for you than that you could– nor nature anything better for you than that you would save as many people as possible."[117]

Similarly in book one of *On Moral Duties*: "They who declare the state publically should hold on to two precepts of Plato: the first is that they should watch over what is to the advantage of the citizenry, so that whoever

---

[113] Aristotle *Nicomachaean Ethics* I. 1094b
[114] Aristotle *Nicomachaean Ethics* I. 1169a
[115] Aristotle *Nicomachaean Ethics* I. 1094a
[116] Aristotle *Topics* VIII. 161a
[117] Cicero *pro Ligario* XII. 38

should agitate, they would inform to him, as sullying their own advantage; the other is that they do not take care of the entire body of the state until they watch over some part that the rest have forsaken."[118]

Similarly, in the *Invective against Salust* he says: "however much someone devotes himself to the state, so much shall he be my friend or my enemy."[119]

Similarly in the book *On Moral Duties*: "splendidly was written by Plato that we are not only born for ourselves; our fatherland claims a share of our life, a part too is claimed by our friends, and, as it pleases the Stoics, since the reason all things are brought forth onto the earth is for man's use, men too are brought forth for the use of others, so that there can be help between them each to the other."[120] The same is said in the *Oration on behalf of the People to the Senate*: "that death is not miserable which is met for the sake of the state nor is that exercise shameful which is performed with virtue."[121] The same is found in the first book of the *Invective*: "my fatherland is by far dearer to me than my life."[122]

Cato too says: "fight for your fatherland."[123]
But for this topic, too this is satisfactory.

3. The same is proven by examples concerning creatures that have only natural love

Concerning creatures that have only natural love: we see that water ascends upwards, contrary to its nature,

---

[118] Cicero *De Oficiis* I. 26
[119] Ps. Cicero *Invectia contra Salustium* IV.11
[120] Cicero *De Oficiis* I. 7
[121] Ps. Cicero *Oratione Populari ad Senatum* IX. 9
122 Cicero *Oratio in Catilinam Prima in Senatu Habita* I.11
[123] Dionysius Cato *Monasticha Catonis* 30

though this does not happen contrary to the nature of the whole universe, that is, that there should not be a vacuum in the universe. This is evident when a lit candle is placed in a basin filled with water under the opening of a phial filled only with air; then, in fact, the water ascends into the phial through this opening, because of the consumption of the air by the fire. Similarly, and for the same reason, air descends in place of the water, just as is evident when a vase full of some other liquid is immersed in water, from which the liquid comes out through the lower opening when an opening is made in the part of the higher vase and immediately air descends into that vase.

For this reason the commentator says in regards to "introducing water into a water clock" in book four of the *Physics*: "In this instrument, water does not flow from the bottom part, when the top part is closed off, but when it is open it flows; this occurs by necessity from the incursion of air into this instrument,"[124] that is when air is able to enter into it; "therefore when air is forced out of it, there does not remain a vacuum, but air rushes in to replace it."[125]

Augustine too, in the second book of *On the Origin of the Soul*, says: "Sink a concave vase, which you believe to be empty, but that you should understand to be full, from that part through which it is filled in water and behold that no liquid is able to enter it, repelled as it is by the air with which it is filled. When, however, it is sunk with the mouth facing upward or toward the side, it accepts the liquid, the air, to which an exit is accessible, exits and

---

[124] Aristotle *Physics* IV. 6: 213a
[125] Ibid

rushes out."[126] From whence, though, is it impossible for water to enter into water in the vase, nor two bodies to be in the same place simultaneously? This is because, so to say, it is against the natural law of the universe. Earth and fire function similarly in the same situations.

4. The same is proven by examples of creatures that have animal love

The same is even apparent in creatures that have animal love. Bees, ignoring labor and danger, incline naturally to the common good. For, as Ambrosius says in the *Exameron*, bees "hold their young in common, they inhabit one house, they are enclosed by one door's threshold. They work together and share their food, each task is done communally, they share enjoyment and their profit, flight and family."[127]

And again: there is no indolence found in in the bee, no matter how close the examination; certain ones contend against other bees in the open, as if in war, others stand guard around their livelihood, others spy out coming rains and seek their origin, others create wax out of flowers, others put together cells, some round and some segmented marvelous in their connection and similarity.[128] Even in the midst of so much different work, not one is taken in ambushed by another, not one searches for food in order to take it, but after flying closer and working among the herbs and flowers, which are their own, he returns and seeks harmony with the others. The same person says that they set up a king for themselves whom

---

[126] Augustine *De Origine Anime ad Vincentium* IV. 18
127 Ambrosius *Exameron* V. 21 (cf. *Patrologia Latina* XIV. 248a)
[128] Ibid (cf. *Patrologia Latina* XIV. 249c-250a)

they hold dear out of natural condition and whom "they defend to the highest degree and for whom they believe to die is glorious,"[129] because it is clear that the king is their head and rules the whole multitude.

5. The same is proved by examples of creatures that have rational love, that is by pagan examples.

The same is clear in those who have rational love, i.e. in humans. When fear strikes the heart, heat and blood leave the other members behind because of natural love and rush to the heart, for its defense. The arms, too, expose themselves to blows for the defense of the head, because, as is clear, the life of the entire body depends on the heart and on the head. Like the arms, the feet, eyes and all of the other members take from themselves and give to the stomach, because on it depends the preservation of the multitude of the body parts, just as is made clear in Aesop's Fable where it says:

No one is satisfied on his own; every friend has need of a friend.

If you are not able to pardon on account of others, pardon on your own account.[130]

Therefore, the honor of every citizen is from the good of the community, as is his exaltation and good.

We see the same thing in humans following rational love, i.e. that of virtue. First concerning pagan examples, we see political virtue. It is said of unnumbered virtuous Romans, that they most frequently exposed themselves to death for the Republic, i.e. for the good of the common

---

[129] Ibid (cf. *Patrologia Latina* XIV. 248-250).
[130] Phaedrus Augustus-Libertus *Fabulae Aesopiae* LV.

public, since they cared for the common good more than for their own.

For the exterior good, we have such a great example of this in Lucius and Quintus, of whom says Augustine in book five of *The City of God* of Lucius Valerius: "who was a so well regarded that when he died a poor man during his consulship, money was collected for his tomb;"[131] and of Quintus Cincinnatus: "When he possessed four igera of land, and cultivated them with his own hands, he was taken from his plow and made dictator, a greater position than that of the consul; following this great honor, after defeating the enemies he remained in the same poverty."[132] These men did not rob the community for their own gain, as do the officials in our own time; for the officials of the community, because they were poor before, are seen enriching themselves without any artifice in office; this is certainly a most terrible sign.

Likewise, we have an example in Fabricius, a poor Roman soldier, who was sent by the Roman people with many others as an ambassador to king Phyrrus, who is descended, as it is said, from the lineage of Achilles, for the return of the captives. He was sought out by a messenger from the king at night and in secret in order to ask him whether he would abandon the Romans and go over to his side, if he would give him a fourth part of his kingdom. The lover of his community responded that he could in no way do this. Afterward, it is said that Phyrrus was defeated by the Romans and that he was wounded.

Afterward, Fabricius, it is said, was made the captain of the Roman army against Pyrrhus, and when the armies

---

[131] Augustine *De Civitate Dei* V. 18
[132] Ibid

were drawing near to each other and because, it is said, Phyrrus was lying down because of these wounds, Phyrrus' doctor came at night in secret to Fabricius, promising to poison the king, if he would give him money. Fabricius captured him, however, and had him bound in chains, and so had him returned to the king and related to him through a messenger what the doctor intended to do. Then said the king: "He is Fabricius, who then was as true to his honesty and faith as the sun is to its course." In this he held forth the good of the community in a similar way.

Valerius, however, says, in book six,[133] that the father of the doctor, Timocrates by name, promised this to Fabricius and that the senate responded and sent legates to Phyrrus that he should be on his guard; he did not, however, reveal the author of the wickedness, but only the crime.

Likewise, it is said in the histories of the Romans (and Valerius touches upon in book five as well)[134] that, after the death of Camillus and two years of plague, a most terrible opening of the earth appeared in the middle of the city with a vast mouth, which was seen to be so deep that it reached even to the underworld. For a long time the populace endured this with great fear. A certain Marcus Curtius, a soldier, armed with all his weapons sprang into this chasm and the mouth was closed up after him, and that the city was freed from such a danger. He had heard that the astrologers and the augurs had agreed that this mouth would not be closed, unless some live man threw

---

[133] Valerius Maximus *Factorum ac Dictorum Memorabilium Libri IX* V. 5

[134] Valerius Maximus *Factorum ac Dictorum Memorabilium Libri IX* V. 6

himself into it; and this was done, and the earth returned to its former state after Marcus threw himself into it, whom no one saw again.

Such a great example of the good concerning the members of the body we have in the king Zaleucus, of whom Valerius says in book six: "although his son was condemned for adultery and ought to be blinded, the entire populace opposed this in honor of the father. Lest he violate the law that he had established, after first taking his own and then his son's eye, Zaleucus left the other so that he could still see."[135] The law therefore pertained to the common good of the people.

Such a great example truly of the bodily good among those who are related we have in Torquatus, of whom Augustine says in book five of *The City of God*: "There was another Roman prince, whose name was Torquatus, who killed his own son, despite his victory, even though he fought, not against his country, but for it, driven by youthful ardor after being taunted by the enemy. He did this because he fought contrary to his command; that is against that which his father, and general, had commanded. There is nothing worse than to be struck down in contempt as an example by the general, nothing better than to be struck down in glory by the enemy."[136] Whence he preferred the greater good of the community to the smaller personal good, since it is written in *Proverbs*: "The obedient man is called victorious."[137] This is certain-

---

[135] Valerius Maximus *Factorum ac Dictorum Memorabilium Libri IX* VI. 5
[136] Augustine *De Civitate Dei* V. 18
[137] *Proverbs* 21:28

ly the normal state, from time to time, however, the inobedient man wins by chance.

Such a great example of the good of the corporal life itself we have in Marcus Regulus, of whom Augustine says in *The City of God*: "Marcus Regulus, a general of the Roman people was made a captive by the Carthaginians. They preferred to have their own returned to them, than to keep their captives, In order to achieve this, they sent this Regulus with their ambassadors to Rome, first they constrained him with a vow, that if this did not occur, he would be returned to Carthage. He hastened, and he persuaded the opposite course in the senate, because he did not think that an exchange of captives was useful for the Roman Republic. Nor was he compelled to return to the enemy from his own people after this, but because he had sworn, he fulfilled it of his own volition. But they put him to death with inventive and horrible tortures. He was enclosed in a narrow wooden box, where he was compelled to stand, fixed on all sides with sharpest nails so that he could lean on no part of it without severest pain, and so they killed him by forcing him to stay awake."[138]

Likewise we have an example in Codrus, of whom Valerius says: "Codrus was king of Athens when the crippled fatherland was laid waste by a vast army of enemies with fire and the sword, because they were mistrustful of human help, they fled to the oracle of Apollo, and through ambassadors asked how he could shatter the enemy in battle; the oracle responded that this would occur only if he himself were killed in battle by the enemies hand. This

---

[138] Augustine *De Civitate Dei* I. 15

was known not only in the Athenian camp, but in the opposing camp as well. Because of this a decree was made that Codrus should not be wounded. He learned of this later, and having set aside the signs of his rank, he put on the clothing of a household servant and exposed himself to the array of enemies, he forced one of these to strike him with a curved blade to his death, so that Athens not be destroyed."[139]

Likewise, says Valerius, when Alexander took the city of Lampsacus by assault, in order to destroy it. He met Anaximenes, his teacher, coming out of the walls, knowing that he would ask him to set aside his anger, he swore that he would not do whatever he asked. "I ask therefore," he said "that Lapsacus be destroyed." And so safety was maintained through the benefit of one oath.[140]

Likewise Cato killed himself, as others suppose, because the possession of the city came to the hands of Julius Caesar, believing because of this that the Republic had fallen into great danger.[141] Augustine, nevertheless, said that Cato did this –as Caesar had said- because he envied the glory of Caesar in such a great way that he did not want to be pardoned by him just as he hoped and wished pardon for his son; and Augustine adds: "or he was ashamed, as we may say in another way more gently,"[142] that is, because he was spared by Caesar.

But this suffices for the present.

---

[139] Valerius Maximus *Factorum ac Dictorum Memorabilium Libri IX* V. 6

[140] Valerius Maximus *Factorum ac Dictorum Memorabilium Libri IX* VII. 3

[141] Plutarch *Cat. Mi.* 70. 6 and Cicero *De Oficiis* I. 31

[142] Augustine *De Civitate Dei* I. 23

6. The Same is proven by the Faithful of the Old Testament.

This is clear in examples of the faithful of both Testaments as well. First let us look in the Old Testament, from which it suffices, for the present, to bring three men who were the most excellent

For it is said of Moses, that he said to the Lord: "I beseech You, Lord, the people have made this greatest sin; they have made for themselves golden gods; remove this stain from them, or, if You cannot, delete me from that book which You have written;"[143] however, because he did this first, twenty three thousand were killed because of this crime, according to one translation, or three thousand, according to another.[144] Certainly God places the majority of the multitude above the minority in the order of love. So that God would spare the remaining majority He made a punishment among the minority and Moses said: "I beseech You, Lord." Etc...

On these words the Magister says in the *Hystories*: "They speak certain words not because of reason, but because of boldness of spirit, saying what is impossible through great confidence in God, as if 'just like it is impossible that you delete me, so, I pray that you cannot abandon me.' Augustine says that the reason must be concluded from the consequences since, certainly, these follow from what is done: 'Either delete me or remove from them.' Since he puts them as equivalent, as if he said: 'If you do not delete me, remove from them.' The disjointed ideas are turned and joined together, destruction, which

---

[143] *Exodus* 32:31-32
[144] *Exodus* 32:28

precedes, and remaining, which follows."[145] And the Magister adds: "It is written in two ways who is to be deleted from the book of life, either according to foreknowledge or following the present justice."[146]

Likewise it is said (concerning David) in first Kings that there existed a young man who, for the liberation of the people of Israel, exposed himself in battle, unarmed, with a most powerful and well-armed giant.[147] Likewise of the same man it is said in second Kings: "When he saw the angel withdrawing from the people he said to the Lord: 'I am the one who sinned, I have done iniquity, what have these people, who are sheep, done? Turn, I pray, Your hand against me and against the house of my father."[148]

Likewise of Judas Maccabeus exposed himself and his brothers to seemingly infinite dangers for the liberation of his people and he did incredible deeds, which are held in first Maccabees.[149] Of this same man can be read in chapter nine that together with eight hundred men[150] he fought against twenty two thousand men,[151] where this most brave man fell fighting, saying: "Far be it from us to do this thing, to flee from them; and if our time draws near, let us die with honor," This how it befits that honorable men die, "for our brothers, and let us not bring judgment on our glory."[152]

---

[145] Petrus Comestor *Historia Scholastica: Libri Exodi* Capitulum LXVII
[146] Ibid
[147] I *Kings* 17: 31-51
[148] II *Kings* 24:17
[149] I *Maccabees* 9:6
[150] I *Maccabees* 9:4
[151] I *Maccabees* 9:10
[152] Ibid

7. The Same is Proven by the Faithful of the Canonical New Testament.

Following these examples from the Old Testament, we shall bring examples from the New Testament as well, and first from the canonical books. Where many must be omitted, the example of two will suffice for us, certainly that of St. Paul, and of Christ our Lord Himself.

Paul says in first *Corinthians*: "Not seeking for what is useful for me, but for many, that they may be saved."[153] And in second *Corinthians*, that: (*Glossa:* I lay out most pleasingly, for your use) "spiritual and temporal things" and: (*Glossa:* I lay this over your souls) "perfect love is this, that one should be ready to die for their brothers."[154]

Again in Romans he says: "I would wish myself to be anathema, (*Glossa:* "if this were possible, that is separate either for an hour, or in this life or after death) from Christ for my brothers, who are my kinsmen according to the flesh, who are Israelites (*Glossa:* "Consider that he said 'I wish' not 'I hope,' since he knows such a one, that is such an honest member, cannot be separated from Christ by any preceding crime, nevertheless he demonstrates affection and concern for them).[155]

Of Christ Himself Paul says in *Hebrews*: "Jesus, in order to sanctify the people with His blood suffered beyond the gates."[156] And Christ says of Himself: "The son of man did not come to be served, but to serve and to give his life as a redemption for many."[157]

---

[153] I *Corinthians* 10:33
[154] II *Corinthians* 12:15
[155] *Romans* 9:3-4
[156] *Hebrews* 13:12
[157] *Matthew* 20:28

8. The Same Proven in the Faithful of the New Testament Outside of the Canon.

Following this up closely, we put examples of other saints from outside the Canon, although omitting so many, it is sufficient to put the example of four, or rather in four, that is in one pope, in one archbishop, in one bishop and in one layman.

It is said in the chronicles of Leo I, the most holy pope, by birth a Tuscan, that when Atilla, the king of the Vandals, was destroying all of Lombardia, lest he do the same coming to Rome, he went personally to meet him in Lombardia, around the Po river, where he was waiting. When he approached, Attila, when saw blessed Leo, dismounted from his horse and having prostrated himself at his feet asked that he request whatever he wished. He asked that he wouold retreat from Italy and that he would return the captives.

To those of his men who accused that the conqueror of the world was defeated by a priest he responded: "I provided for myself and for you. For I saw standing on his right hand a most puissant warrior with bared sword threatening me and saying: 'If you do not obey him, you will be destroyed with all your host.'" From there he immediately exited Italy and returned to Pannonia. So, then, God gives virtue and protection to those who expose themselves to peril for the good of the many.

Again, it is said of blessed Thomas the Archbishop of Canterbury, who wished rather to die than that the liberty of the church be infringed upon, that, hastening to death, when armed men were searching for him he said: "I am he, what do you wish?" and they said: "We wish that you would die and not be able to live any longer." To them he said: "I am ready to die for God and for the de-

fense of justice and for the liberty of the church. If, therefore, you are searching for me, I prohibit you on behalf of
God almighty and under anathema from injuring any of
these others in any way."

Again, it is said of blessed Lupus, bishop of Trecassinus, that when his city was besieged by Attila, blessed
Lupus asked, shouting from above the gates, who this
may be who attacks them so. To this he said: "I am Attila,
the scourge of God." To this the humble defender said,
sighing: "And I am Lupus, alas destroyer of the flock of
God." Soon he commanded that the gates be opened. They
however passed from gate to gate, blinded by divinity,
neither seeing nor harming anyone.

Again, blessed Ludovicus, king of the Franks, exposed
himself and his sons and brothers to innumerable dangers
and expenses for the defense of the Holy land and the
Christian people. For after returning from his first voy-
age across the sea, where he was made captive by the Saracens, nevertheless he returned for a second time, and he
died a blessed death.

9. The same is proven by arguments made with respect to the object; that is, to those things which are loved naturally by all.

This proposition becomes clear in a number of different arguments as well. First: in an argument made with
respect to the object, or from all things loved naturally.
Second: through an argument made with respect to the
subject, which is men who love. Third: an argument made
with respect to the causes of love. Fourth: an argument
made with respect to the effects of love. Fifth: an argument made with respect to the signs of love.

Concerning the first argument, it must be noted that, for the present purpose, there are five things which seem to be loved naturally by all, that is: the good of the community, beauty, being, God and happiness.

Of the first, the philosopher says in the first book of the *Ethics* that philosophers: "reported well the good which all desired;"[158] and he says the same in many other places, Dionysius too says as much in the fourth chapter of *On the Divine Names*.[159] From this certainly follows that the good of the community is to be loved more than the good of any individual, since the good of the community has more in common with the highest good than the individual good – both are called common through a kind of uncertainty – it follows then that the common is a greater good than the individual since the particular is included in the common as such, and not vice versa.

Regarding the second, that is regarding beauty, Dionysius says in chapter four of *On the Divine Names* that beauty is loveable by all;[160] and in *Song of Songs* is said: "you are beautiful, my beloved."[161] From this undoubtedly follows that any citizen should prefer the common good of the city over his own good and any Christian the common good of the universal church over his own private good, since the total beauty of a part, in however many parts it is, depends on the beauty of the whole. This is seen in two ways.

First, because the part, which is counted beautiful considered for itself alone, if it should not come together

---

[158] Aristotle *Nicomachean Ethics* I. 1094a

[159] Ps. Dionysius the Areopagyte *De Divinis Nominibus* IV. 7

[160] Ibid

[161] *Song of Songs* 1:15

with the whole is ugly, as Augustine says in book three of the *Confessions*: "Ugly is every part that is not united with its whole."[162] Of this we have an example both in the human body and in architecture. The nose, whether or not it is beautiful in and of itself, is ugly if it does not correspond with the size of the face. The same is true of the face in respect to the rest of the body. The same is also true of a plaza in respect to the city or to the castle and of a cloister or dormitory or other building in respect to the entire monastery. For, according to the Philosopher and to Dionysius, beauty consists in proportionality, without which it cannot exist.

Where, therefore, can the citizen or the Christian be beautiful with the flower of prosperity if his city or the church is withered, oppressed, destroyed? This is not possible. A flower is beautiful in the meadow, not in dung or in the manure pile. Second. This is again made apparent by the same reasoning, since a part, which on its own seems ugly, is made more beautiful when considered as part of a whole, this is seen in Augustine *Enchiridion*: "The wonderful beauty of the universe derives from all things, in which even that which is called wicked, arranged well and put in its proper place, augments the good since they please more greatly and are more praiseworthy when compared to wickedness."[163]

We have an example of this in paintings, in which the colors black and ashen, although they are ugly in and of themselves, are beautiful as a part of the whole painting. The same is true in palaces, in which the fetid places, that is, the stables and the privy, are made beautiful. This even

---

[162] Augustine *Confessions* II. 8
[163] Augustine *Enchiridion* III. 11

holds true in the human body, in which the excretory and pubic parts are considered beautiful.

Therefore, a citizen, however poor he may be, should engage himself that his community flourish because from this he will himself flourish. Therefore, since the individual good relates itself to the common good just like the part to the whole, it follows that the common good must be loved more.

As to the third matter, that is, as to existence, the Philosopher says in book nine of the *Ethics* that existence is naturally "desired and loved by all;"[164] indeed, as Augustine also says in book three of *On Free Will*, that nothing can wish not to exist.[165] From this doubtlessly follows two things concerning our subject. It follows first that the whole has more of existence than the part because the whole, since it is the whole, has existence in actuality, the part, since it is the part, does not have existence except potentially. As the Philosopher says in book seven of the *Physics*, that which exists only potentially is not being itself, but entirely follows that which is, as the Philosopher also discusses in book one of the *Physics*.[166]

This same principle follows secondly as well, since the existence of the part, such as it has, depends on the existence of the whole. The part existing beyond the whole is no longer a part, as it was called while it was part of the whole. The hand, when it is cut off, is not a hand, except metaphorically, just as, for instance, stone or painted ones, as is made clear by the Philosopher in book two of

---

[164] Aristotle *Nicomachean Ethics* IX. 1168a
[165] Augustine *De Libero Arbitrio* III. 8
[166] Aristotle *Physics* VII. 5: 250a 22-24

On the Soul,[167] in book eight of the *Metaphysics*[168] and in book one of the *Politics*,[169] the hand does not have the ability to operate independently, for example to sense what is being touched, to bring food to the mouth, to cut and other such things.

Again, the existence of a part depends on the existence of the whole, and not vice versa, just as the hindmost depends on that which comes before it and not vice versa; hence the Philosopher says in book one of the *Politics* "the city stands before the home and before each one of us; for it is necessary that the whole stands before the part. The foot will not exist if the whole is destroyed, nor will the hand, except metaphorically, just as if someone should call it (a hand) made of stone; such a thing will be destroyed. All things are defined by their function and virtue; for this reason, if they no longer serve this function they can in no way be called this, except metaphorically,"[170] since these things are lacking in the operation and virtue by which they are defined, as the definition of the foot is that it is the organic member having the virtue to allow walking.

Because of the destruction of the state, the citizen remains as if stone or painted, since he certainly lacks the operation and virtue which he had before: the soldier in military matters, the merchant in selling, the artist in the carrying out of his art, the official in his office, the head of the family in family affairs and the universally free man in his freedom, that is in going to visit his holdings,

---

[167] Aristotle *De anima* II. 1 412b 20-22
[168] Aristotle *Metaphysics* VII. 1035b
[169] Aristotle *Politics* I. 1253a
[170] Ibid

in making embassies, in having dominion over foreign cities and suchlike.

As he who was a Florentine citizen, because of the destruction of Florence is no longer to be called a Florentine, but rather a weeper.[171] And if he is not a citizen he is not a human, since a human is naturally a political animal, following what the Philosopher says in book eight of the *Ethics*[172] and in the first book of the *Politics*.[173]

Regarding the fourth point, that is regarding God, the Philosopher says in book two of *On the Soul* that everything strives for divinity "and for this reason they do that which they do according to their nature."[174] *Proverbs* states too: "The Lord has created all for Himself:"[175] for Himself, that is to say He is the one who is to be striven for and participated in, according to what is possible for each creature, as its station allows. The rational creature is able to participate in God above other creatures that it even deserves to be called god through virtue and grace, as is seen in *John* "He gave to them the power to become sons of God, to these who believed in His name;"[176] and in second *Peter*: "He gave a great and precious promise to us, that through this we may be made partakers in the divine nature,"[177] (*Glossa*: through grace) through which they knew and loved Him. All other creatures in essence or by living are made more similar, more or less, to God, since

---

[171] A Flerentine
[172] Aristotle *Nicomachean Ethics* VIII. 11622a
[173] Aristotle *Politics* I. 1253a (Latin text attributes this to Aristotle's *Physics*).
[174] Aristotle *De Anima* II. 415b 1-2
[175] *Proverbs* 16:4
[176] *John* 1:12
[177] II *Peter* 1:4

God turns all things to Himself as to the final end, just as Dionysius says in *On the Divine Names.*[178]

From this follows the same point as before, since the common good has a greater similarity with God than the good of a private individual does, since God is striven for by all in a community, as was said, since all things are communally in Him, who is the perfection of all creatures, as is said in *Exodus*: "I will extend to you every good thing,"[179] also since He is Himself communally in all creatures, as is said in first *Corinthians*: "So God may be all in all,"[180] and since He is the common cause of all, in creating them, as is said in *John*: "All things were made through Him,"[181] and in conserving them, as is said in *Hebrews*: "Carrying all things by His word of virtue,"[182] and in providing for them, as is said in *The Wisdom of Solomon*: "You, however, Father, govern every foresight."[183] He Himself is the one who communally "makes His sun to shine on the good and the wicked and He rains over the just and the unjust," as is said in *Matthew*: "Nor is there anyone who may conceal himself from His heat,"[184] as is said in *Psalm* 18,[185] that is from his help and favor.

From all this is manifestly shown that however much more participation one has in the divine so much love one has for the community. The Philosopher connects greater divinity with greater love for the community well in the

---

[178] Ps. Dionysius the Areopagyte *De Divinis Nominibus* IV. 4
[179] *Exodus* 33:19
[180] I *Corinthians* 15:28
[181] *John* 1:3
[182] *Hebrews* 1:3
[183] *The Wisdom of Solomon* 14:3
[184] *Matthew* 5:45
[185] *Psalm* 18:7

first book of the *Ethics*, where he says: "Certainly to be loved are the affairs of one man, truly better and more divine is that of the whole people and of the state;"[186] Augustine speaks similarly when he says: "However much more you are concerned for the community than for your own interests, so much more advancement will you come to know,"[187] that is in the love for God and in becoming more similar to Him.

Regarding the fifth point, that is regarding happiness, the Philosopher says in many places, as do Augustine and Boethius and many other saints, that everyone naturally seeks happiness. The same conclusion follows from the fact that perfect happiness is not possible in only one human, but is pushed outward for this reason, that the good may be participated in by many. The Philosopher discusses this in book nine of the *Ethics*: "It is unsuitable, as it happens, to make this happy man solitary. Assuredly no one would choose that he alone have every good; for man is communal and born adapted to coexist with others;"[188] from which he also says that the happy man requires friends with whom he may live and with whom he may be delighted in living with them and whom he may benefit.

What's more, happiness, as it is perfect according to its nature, cannot exist when nature is found to be deficient; and so the Philosopher says in book nine of the *Ethics*: the happy man "has those things which are good by nature;"[189] but naturally men love their homeland, in which

---

[186] Aristotle *Nicomachean Ethics* I. 1094b
[187] Augustine *Regula* Caput V: 31
[188] Aristotle *Nicomachean Ethics* IX. 1169b
[189] Ibid

they were born, as the saying goes: "its own nest is beautiful to each bird;" and Ovid says:

> The sweet love of country is stronger than any reason. I do not know how birth alone drives everyone together because of is sweetness nor allow their own to be forgotten. What is better than Rome? What worse than frigid Scythia? Nevertheless from that city the barbarian fled here.[190]

From these things it is clear that the natural love for fatherland defeats the natural love for the individual person since a person even chooses to be there when there is risk to their person, just as is seen in many of our own citizens bereft of health and of fertile offspring. Therefore if someone puts the private love of his own person above the love for his fatherland, clearly he does this against his nature and because of this he does it against the natural order.

10. The same is proven with respect to the subject, that is, with respect to humans who love.

This proposition remains to be proven by arguments made with respect to the subject of love that is from men who love. Every man naturally loves those who are more closely related to him, for instance he loves himself more than those around him and among those around him he loves his kinsmen more than strangers and among his kinsmen he loves his son more than his brother and his brother more than his nephew; and in this way love always decreases the more remote it gets. The same holds true for fire, to which love can be equated, the closer one

---

[190] Ovid *Ex Ponto* I. 3 29, 35-38

is to it, the more it warms. But the whole is more completely joined to the part than the part to itself. Therefore etc...[191]

This proves the lesser point,[192] since the principal and cause of each thing exists within it, and most especially when it is the cause not only of the things origin, but also of its preservation, since that which preserves is stronger that that which founds and causes it. It happens that the son is stronger than the father, who is the principle and cause of the son. Nor is the father the cause of the preservation of substance for the son, since the son, having lost his father in death, nevertheless can be preserved in existence.

The relationship which the part has with itself is caused by the relationship which the part has with the whole, and it is preserved by this since the part, beyond the existence of the whole, does not exist, as is seen from what was said before. Since, then, it does not exist, it cannot be joined with anything, neither with itself nor with anything else, since joining presupposes existence just as also all other created things, for example life, size, health, friendship, conversation, being ill of fever etc..., since "existence is the first of the created things," as it is said in the book *On the Causes.*[193] Therefore the relationship of the whole to the part stands greater than that of the part to itself.

---

[191] Therefore the whole is more to be loved by the part than the part by itself.
[192] That the whole is more joined to the part than the part to itself.
[193] Ps. Aristotle *De Causis* proposition II.

11. The same is proven with respect to the cause of his love, that cause without which it does not exist.

The same concept can be proven with an argument made with respect to the cause of love itself. First: in the argument concerning the cause, without which it is not possible for anything to be loved. Second: in the argument dealing with the reasons which move men to love.

Concerning the first point it must be noted that relationship is that cause without which we cannot love, as Augustine says in the tenth book of *On the Trinity*: "we are able to love separated from each other, but never unknown to each other."[194] But the part, in as much as it is a part, naturally knows the whole better than itself. Therefore, and as a consequence to this, it loves the whole more according to its nature since the intensity of love naturally follows from the intensity of the knowledge, just as it will also be in the glory of the saints, which is not contrary to nature, but rather, a perfected nature.

For the present, however, the fact that it can be said that the part has a greater knowledge of the whole than of itself can be shown in three ways.

1. The part knows the whole before it knows itself. This follows the Philosopher, who said in book one of the *Physics*: "These things are evident to us first and, while they are certainly greatly confused at first, later, however, there arise out of these the known elements and principles through our divisions."[195] That which we know first naturally is also what we will know better. This is manifest in these

---

[194] Augustine *De Trinitate* X. VIII. 11.
[195] Aristotle *Physics* I.1: 184a.

things which are first with respect to nature; just as in the first principles of mathematics, which are also spoken of by the Philosopher in book one of the *Posterior Analytics,* saying that we know the principles better than the conclusions, since "that which belongs to one thing on account of another belongs even more to that other."[196]

This is seen in those things which are most important, as far as we are concerned, that is, in things that are perceptible with the intellect, in the pure sense, as there are things which are most important with regard to nature. "Just as the eye of the bat or of the night bird or of the night heron acts in the light of the sun, so our intellect acts to those things which are manifest in nature," as it is stated in the first books of the *Metaphysics.*[197] But this is seen also in natural things themselves, since because something is known before, it is known for a longer time if it should not be delivered over to oblivion.

The community, as the whole that was known before, is not destroyed through the knowledge of the part. But, because it remains known for a long time, it is strengthened greatly in knowledge, since through familiarity it

---

[196] i.e.Than that which derives from it. Aristotle *Posteriorum Analyticum* I.2:72a.
[197] Aristotle *Metaphysics* II. 993b.

becomes a habit and part of nature, as the Philosopher says in the work *the Categories*: "These things which touch upon us for a long time are impressed into the nature of each person, this is called habit."[198] Therefore since it is known first in a certain manner it is known better.

2. The part knows itself more easily. It is easier for something to be known imperfectly than perfectly and diminishedly, rather than according to the whole. But to know the part according to that which is in the whole is to know the whole incompletely. Therefore it is easier to know the whole as a whole in confusion than the whole according to its individual parts. But, because the part is more easily recognizable by us, we naturally know it better, this is because of the fault of our intelligence, since it does not generally approach difficult things of this type, because of the fault of our soul, which naturally flees from this type of difficulty, seeking quiet more than work.

3. Nevertheless, the part knows the whole more certainly. This follows from the two previous examples. Certainly the whole, insofar as it is somewhat confused, may be more uncertain in itself than its distinct parts, nevertheless it is more certain in respect to our knowledge, we

---

[198] Aristotle *Predicamentorum* VIII. 9a.

who know defectively. For, seeing many coins together at once, I recognize the sum more certainly than the distinct coins which are in the whole. I also recognize the number of persons, or some other things, which are gathered, be it seventy or eighty of them, more clearly than I recognize the individual people who are gathered. As the Philosopher says in book two of *On the Soul:* "assuredly it is from uncertain things" that is according to nature, "that are more obvious, however" that is to us, "that we arrive at that which is more certain and more noted according to reason."[199] Etc...

Hence, although the whole is more uncertain, according to nature considered generally, nevertheless it is more certain as concerns our nature; just as wine simply is sounder than tisane according to the nature of drinks, however tisane simply is certainly sounder for the nature of one who is sick. And in this what the Philosopher says in the sixth book of the *Topics* can perhaps be verified, where he says that *genus* and differences are simply superior and more evident than *species*," certainly *genus* is more common in respect to *species*.[200] The way we distinguish "simply," is discussed in the treatise *On the Nature of Things*.[201]

These things for the present have been discussed, although certainly they may be able to endure misrepresentation.

---

[199] Aristotle *De Anima* II. 2413a: 11-12.
[200] Aristotle *Topicorum* VI. 4. 141b: 27-28.
[201] Here he refers to one of his own works, the *De Modis Rerum.*

12. The same is proven with respect to the cause of motion, especially with respect to virtue.

Now we shall look at this proposition with respect to the causes which naturally move humans to the love of others, of these causes we shall bring up four for the present, these are: virtue, physical attraction, temporal use and similarity.

It must be noted, that the virtue existing in every person, whether it may be intellectual virtue such as wisdom and prudence or moral virtue such as forgiveness, generosity, bravery, justice, mercy and other such virtues, is the cause that naturally moves humans to the love of another human, that is a good one, according to the nature of reason. This is certainly so, since in reason is intellectual virtue, just as in the subject, and from this arises moral virtue, just as from the cause, this is shown by the Philosopher in the *Nicomachean Ethics*.[202] Concerning this Ovid writes in his *From Pontus*: "The idea of friendship naturally moves barbarian hearts."[203]

Friendship is, however, to be spoken of when some one loves another according to the virtue which he possesses, as the Philosopher says in the eighth book of the *Nicomachean Ethics*.[204] Tullius too says in book one of the *On the Nature of the Gods*: "nothing is more to be loved than virtue, and he who will obtain this will be esteemed by us, of whatever nation he may be."[205] Fame alone, even if it is not visible physically, makes the virtuous man to be loved naturally, because of which Augustine and Hieronymus, who, although they never saw each other in the

---

[202] Aristotle *Nicomachean Ethics* I. 1103a.

[203] Ovid *Ex Ponto* III.2: 100.

[204] Aristotle *Nicomachean Ethics* VIII. 1156b.

[205] Cicero *De Natura Deorum* I. XLIV: 120-122.

flesh, still loved each other greatly; whence Augustine wrote to Hieronymus: "If, therefore, we do not know you, since we have not seen your face, in the same way you do not know us, for you also have not seen me."[206] This too this occurs in many other places as well.

From this argument is apparent that the citizen naturally prefers the city over himself since there exists a greater abundance both of intellectual virtue and of moral virtue, or even theological, than in one citizen, since there is more virtue of every type, and even greater, therein than there is in himself, so that he should subordinate himself; since the citizen can be made more virtuous in every way, speaking politely, in conjunction with the state than existing on his own.

Intellectually, since on his own he can acquire wisdom through discovery, but in a community he can also acquire it through discipline. This is even more the case when there are many learned men in the large city, here, through mutual exercise with other students, he can make greater progress. If he should happen to be a learned man, he benefits others by teaching them, since "science is the noble possession of the soul, and it grows by being distributed" etc., has been expertly said.

In the community too, one person is able to help another in those things which are necessary for wisdom; that is to say in intelligence, in memory, in books, in expenses and in other such things, in so far as one has that which another person lacks. "Two people coming together are more able both in their thinking and acting," as is said in book eight of the *Nicomachaean Ethics*;[207] alt-

---

[206] Augustine *Epistula* 40. caput I.
[207] Aristotle *Nicomachean Ethics* VIII. 1155a.

hough a man, insofar as he lives superhumanly, may be more apt to wisdom living alone rather than in company, as is seen in the tenth book of the *Nicomachaean Ethics*.[208]

As to morality; a man in a community can be made more virtuous and even theological, since he is more spurred on to virtue and to good works by the examples of other virtuous men, as is discussed in *Ecclesiastes*. "If two sleep together, they are both kept warm, how shall one be made warm?"[209] he can also be sustained in the good through many temptations, as is discussed in *Ecclesiastes*. "And if someone defeats one, two are able to resist him; a triple cord is difficult to break"[210] should he fall in sin he has those who would lift him up, as is discussed in *Ecclesiastes*. "Alas the solitary man, since when he will fall, he has no one to raise him up;"[211] since virtue both moral and theological are increased through these works.

The person who does these things for others rather than for himself seems far more generous, just, prudent and, even, more loving. For which reason the Philosopher says in the tenth book of the *Nicomachaean Ethics*. "The just man certainly needs those for whom he can work justly and with whom he can work justly; the same holds true for the temperate man, the brave man and each one of the others;"[212] the Lord too in *Luke* says: "No one lights a lamp and puts it in concealment, but above the candelabrum, so that those who enter may see the light."[213] The

---

[208] Aristotle *Nicomachean Ethics* X. 1177a.
[209] *Ecclesiastes* 4:11.
[210] *Ecclesiastes* 4:12.
[211] *Ecclesiastes* 4:10.
[212] Aristotle *Nicomachean Ethics* X. 1177a.
[213] *Luke* 11:33.

infusion of love itself, which is certainly from God, is made a regular disposition by our work, which is done better by the many than by the individual, as is said in *Matthew*: "Where two or three will be gathered in my name, there I am in their midst."[214]

13. The Same is Proven with Respect to Physical Attraction.

The second cause which moves men to love others is physical attraction, and this arises from the nature of the senses because of which a man delights in fairness and in bodily beauty, as it says in *Ecclesiastes*: "the eye desires grace and beauty."[215] Such love is especially prevalent in the youth, in whom the passions dominate the most, as is discussed by the Philosopher in the eighth book of the *Nicomachean Ethics*: "the friendship of young people seems to be because of pleasure. These young people live according to their passions and they pursue that which delights them at that time."[216] Following this natural inclination, the citizen prefers the city to himself.

First of all, according to this nature, that which is more beautiful is more loved. The beauty of the state exceeds the beauty of each individual citizen, since there are many beautiful people there, and this beauty is more intense, since the beauty of the part depends on the beauty of the whole, even should the part be ugly on its own, as is discussed above. The beauty of an entire field in bloom is greater than that of one individual flower, since it is more beautiful according to both of these ways discussed.

---

[214] *Matthew* 18:20.
[215] *Ecclesiastes* 40:22.
[216] Aristotle *Nicomachean Ethics* VIII. 1156a.

Secondly, this holds true since that which is loved by the whole citizenry is more beloved by the individual citizen than that which is beloved by him alone. Just as the existence of the part depends on the whole, as was said, so do all other things which follow existence and that which presupposes it, just like the fairness and the beauty so even the pleasantness of the part depends on the pleasantness of the whole. Therefore just as the part that is incongruent with the whole cannot have beauty, neither can it have natural pleasantness.

What kind of pleasantness can the Florentine citizen have, seeing the sad state of his city, filled with greatest sorrow? For the plazas are deplazad, that is they are emptied; the house is destroyed, the families are battered; the kinfolk are estranged; the comforts are discomfited; the games seem to have been played, that is lost; the dignities seem resented, that is by the statesmen and captains who have left the city; the offices seem bewitched, that is under a spell, the priory, the embassies and suchlike; the farms are laid waste, since the trees are torn out, the vines are cut down, the palaces are destroyed and it is not possible, that is one cannot, live in them any more or go to them without fear and trembling.

Finally, the flower is wilted and the scent of fame is turned into the horrible odor of infamy, this fulfills the prophecy of its own name among the vulgar people, for they do not call it "Fiorenza" as foreign people do, but "Firenze." The French, when they come across dung, or some other fetid thing, they say: "fi fi" holding their nose, as if to say: "O how much this stinks!" Thus Florence is changed into Flerence, the city of tears. Therefore every citizen weeps because of natural love for Florence.

14. The Same is Proven with Respect to Temporal Utility.

The third cause which naturally moves men to love others is utility, this arises out of imperfect or defective nature. For all men are naturally defective, as is discussed in *Psalm 72*: "my flesh lacks, as does my heart."[217] This type of love is especially found in the old, who are greatly afflicted with difficulties, and nature already forsakes them; whence the Philosopher says in book eight of the *Nicomachean Ethics*: "This friendship seems to exist mostly in the old, for they do not seek what is delightful, but what is useful."[218]

But all men seem to love because of usefulness alone, as is discussed in *Proverbs*: "The wealthy have many friends;"[219] and Seneca says: "honey is followed by flies, grain by ants, bodies by wolves, this crowd follows spoils, not a man."[220] Thus even the pagans loved Christ as is said of Tiberius the emperor, that he loved Jesus, desiring to be cured of leprosy by Him, as he was healed later through His kindness.

Christians too love Saracens or Jews, through whom they gain profit, and the converse holds true as well. In the same way, even a city will love another because of assistance in war and other mutually rendered aid. Because of this too the citizen loves his city more than himself. The use of the part depends on the use of the whole, just as was true of existence and the consequences of existence, as was discussed above.

---

[217] *Psalm 72 (73): 26.*
[218] Aristotle *Nicomachean Ethics* VIII. 1156a.
[219] *Proverbs 14:20*
[220] Ps. Seneca *De Remediis Fortuitorum* X.4.

This is also shown by the fact that humans naturally join together and create a city, or some other community for the use of each individual, that the defects of human life may be overcome, which one alone could not overcome, that one may supplement where another is lacking, since one makes shoes, another houses, another clothing, another ploughs the ground, another makes arms, and so those things which human life needs comes from many.

No one is enough on his own, every friend has need of a friend. If you do not wish to spare others, spare yourself, just as Aesop says of the limbs and the stomach, which was discussed above.

What type of use can the Florentine citizen have? The societies are dissolute, the foundations – so to speak – are broken up, the workshops are abandoned, that is at rest and empty, the artists are disarticulated, the merchants are made weak, the doctors are made indigent, the laws are bound up, the courts are reduced, the labors are undone, the guild houses are free, that is abandoned, the neighbors are estranged, the like minded are in disagreement, friends have become enemies, every faithful person has become faithless, hearts are broken, and have become cruel, the willing have become bewitched, the compatriots have become estranged so that because of the destruction of the city already an individual citizen can be useful for himself or for anyone else, instead brings harm.

And so well, that is badly, "Florence" is changed to "Firenze." Once, because of the scent of its fame, strangers from far off places deposited their money for temporal uses and for monetary profit, now, however, because of the stench of infamy, even the Florentines themselves attempt to carry away from there those things which they deposit and – which is more awful – they cannot regain what is theirs.

15. The Same is Proven with Respect to Similarity.

The fourth reason which brings men naturally to love others is similarity, as is discussed in *Ecclesiastes*: "Every creature loves that which is similar to it;"[221] and the Philosopher says in the eighth book of the *Nicomachean Ethics*: "like helps like and crows help crows."[222] This arises from the nature of an entity, since every creature is an entity by nature.

Since, then, every creature naturally loves itself, it naturally loves everything in which it sees itself; and however much more it is present and however closer it is, so much more does it love it according to natural inclination; so, for example, the love by which a weighty object existing in its own place loves another existing in a similar place is greater than for one existing in a different place, since an entity in actuality is better than a potential entity.

For this reason the love of friendship, which is for a fully realized thing, is greater and more powerful than the love of something longed for, which one has for something that exists only potentially. Since being in actuality is being without complication, being in potential is being according to what it could be, as is discussed by the Philosopher in the first book of the *Physics*;[223] just as an egg is, without complication, an egg but an animal according to what it could be.

---

[221] *Ecclesiastes* 13:19.
[222] Aristotle *Nicomachean Ethics* VIII. 1155a
[223] Aristotle *Physics* I.8: 191b 13-19.

The proximity which exists within a type (genus) is greater than that within an entity, and that which is in the type (genus) subordinate to the community is greater still, and that which is in the species is greater still, and that which is in the substance is greater than that in the accident; and therefore a human loves the animate, such as a tree, more than the inanimate, such as a rock, and animals or birds more than trees, and humans more than animals and kinfolk more than people of the same color or the same language.

Because of this natural inclination the citizen loves the city more than himself, because of the greater similarity which the part has to the whole than it has to itself. This is so, since the part has existence only potentially, as it is a part, as was discussed above, while the whole, as it is a whole, has existence in actuality. So, however great the proximity of the part is to itself so much greater is the proximity of the part to the whole, since this proximity depends on it, just like the entity itself does, without which no proximity is possible since existence is communal.

16. The Same is Proven by an Argument Made in Respect to the Effects of Love.

It remains to discuss the argument made in respect to the effects of love, of which, for the present, we will discuss five examples.

The first of these effects is the uniting of the lover with his beloved (this occurs even if they may be distant), either formally, according to the affect, since love is in a certain sense a union, or effectively according to fact, as marriage joins formally, but those being married join each other effectively. This follows what Dionysius says in chapter four of *On the Divine Names*: "we understand that love, be it natural, animal, rational or intellectual, is a unifying virtue."[224]

Augustine too says in book eight of his *On the Trinity*: "Love is life joining two different people or striving to join them, that is the one who loves and the one who is loved."[225] That he says "joining," refers to the union of the affected, which certainly is love in essence, since the souls of friends are as one. The Philosopher says this as well in book nine of the *Nicomachean Ethics*; that he truly says "strives to join them"[226] pertains to the actual union, through which it is possible without corruption to become one from two, since they speak together, share together, abide together and suchlike; whence the Philosopher says in book two of the *Politics* that lovers desire to become one from two.[227]

From this argument can be concluded that the citizen naturally loves the city over himself, since certainly the union of the part to the whole is greater than that of the part to itself. This is because the first is a union of an entity in actuality, while the second is a union of a potential entity only; and again since this union is caused by the first. The greater love makes the greater union.

The second effect of love is mutual indwelling, because of which the lover is in the beloved and vice versa, just as is discussed in first *John*: "He who abides in love abides in God, and God in him."[228] This happens in two

---

[224] Ps. Dionysius the Areopagyte *De Divinis Nominibus* c.4: 15.
[225] Augustine *De Trinitate* VIII.10: 4-6.
[226] Aristotle *Nicomachean Ethics* IX. 1168b.
[227] Aristotle *Politics* II.4: 1262b 12-13.
[228] I *John* 4:16.

ways: in the first as touches thought, the second as touches desire.

In the first case, it is said that the beloved is in the lover in so far as the one who is loved stays in the thought of the lover, as is discussed in *Phillipians*. "...since I will have all of you in my heart."[229] Conversely, the one who loves is said to be in the beloved in so far as it does not suffice for him to know the outer self of the beloved, but to press on into the inner self and to examine it, that is to the secret heart, as Gregory says. It is said in first *Corinthians* that "he searches the depths of God."[230]

In the second case it is said that the beloved is in the lover because of the interest in their affect; and the lover in the beloved, in so far as the lover seeks to possess the beloved perfectly as if entering into his very center, according to the love of desire. It is said that the love of friendship is in him insofar as he considers the will of his friend as his own. Because of this it is proper for friends to want or not to want the same things and to mourn and rejoice in the same things, as the Philosopher says in the ninth book of the *Nicomachean Ethics*[231] and in the second book of the *Rhetoric*.[232]

For this reason, the part loves the whole more than itself, since certainly the part is in the whole and vice versa, as is discussed by the Philosopher in the fourth book of the *Physics*.[233] The part, however, is not individual in itself, according to the same place in the writings of the

---

229 *Phillipians* 1:7.
230 I *Corinthians* 2:10.
231 Aristotle *Nicomachean Ethics* IX. 1166a.
232 Aristotle *Rethoricae* II.4: 1381a.
233 Aristotle *Physics* IV.3: 210a 15-17.

Philosopher. Nothing can exist in itself on account of the first accident, but it is said that the whole exists in itself in so far as its part is in another part, like wine in an amphora. This is so unless, by chance, existence in itself is understood according to a negation, so, for example, God, who is the most primal, is said to exist in and of Himself in so far as He is not in another. What's more, if the part is said in another way to exist in itself, then it has that which makes it a whole, since in no other way could it be a part.

The third effect of love is ecstasy, that is it puts a human outside of himself, as is discussed Dionysius in chapter four of his *On the Divine Names* "Divine love creates ecstasy."[234] Every love is like a participation in divine love. Love that is criminal is no true love, as is said by Dionysius in chapter four of *On the Divine Names* that corporal love "is not true love, but its mere reflection, or a fallen form of true love."[235]

Therefore, this ecstasy or alienation exists differently in sinful love than it does in natural or divine love, which perfects natural love. In sinful love a human goes beyond himself to that which is below nature or contrary to natural love, since "every sin is contrary to nature, even the nature of that in which the sin exists," as Augustine says in book three of *On Free Will*.[236] In a natural love a man goes beyond himself toward that which is proper according to the nature of the lover, either toward a nature like to his own or to a superior one. In divine love the man

---

[234] Ps. Dionysius the Areopagyte *De divinis nominibus* c. 4 13.
[235] Ps. Dionysius the Areopagyte *De divinis nominibus* c. 4 12.
[236] Augustine *De Libero Arbitrio* III.13:49-50.

goes beyond himself to that which transcends his own nature.

Therefore, sinful love vilifies the lover, as is said in *Hosea*: "they were made abominable, just like that which they loved."[237] But natural love, which loves a nature like itself, makes the lover more noble, as if it were his perfection. Natural love which loves a nature greater than itself ennobles like an even greater perfection, since that citizen has greater nobility who is the manservant of the king or the pope than the one who is free in his own house. The ocean too, because of natural love, in the ebb and flow of the tides, follows the superior nature of the moon more than it does its own nature, in a similar fashion the sun, in its daily rhythm follows the nature of the firmament.

Divine love, however, has the greatest ability to make noble, as is said in *Colossians*: "having love above all, which is the chain of perfection."[238] Therefore a man, because of natural love, seeks good for his superiors, that is for his community, more than for himself; and because of the supernatural affinity for love he follows the commands of God much more than those of his community, if the community acts contrary to the will of God, as is said in *Exodus*: "you should not follow the mob in doing ill."[239]

The fourth effect of love is zeal, as Dionysius says in chapter four of *On the Divine Names*.[240] God is called zealous on account of the great love He has for creation. Certainly, on account of this zeal, the lover hates everty-

---

[237] *Hosea* 9:10.
[238] *Colossians* 3:14.
[239] *Exodus* 23:2.
[240] Ps. Dionysius the Areopagyte *De divinis nominibus* c.4. 13.

thing which goes against his beloved. For this reason someone is said to be zealous for a friend, for faith and even for God when he attempts to keep away, as much as he is able to, that which goes against the good of his friend, the integrity of the faith and the will and honor of God, as is said in first *Kings*.[241] "With zeal I am zealous for God, the Lord of hosts, since the children of Israel have broken their covenant with God;" for which reason the *Glossa* for *John*: "the zeal of your house has consumed me" says concerning good zeal: "he is consumed who works diligently to correct whatever depravity he sees, and he tolerates them with tears if he is unable to."[242]

For this reason the citizen must naturally strive more to remove ills that affect the whole city than those that affect him alone, since the ill of the part is more associated with the ill of the whole than with its own, since through this the part is robbed of its highest good, seeing as through the ill of the whole the part not only loses actual good but the very cause of good, but through a personal ill it is deprived of a potential good and that which is caused by it.

The fifth effect of love is to preserve the lover, as Dionysius says in chapter four of *On the Divine Names*: "a single person loves themselves continuously"[243] that is preservatively. It is certain fom what was said that the part is better preserved by the whole than it is by itself.

There are also many other effects of love, but these suffice for the present.

---

[241] Text has III *Kings* 19:10

[242] *John* 2:17

[243] Ps. Dionysius the Areopagyte *De Divinis Nominibus* c.4: 10.

17. The Same is Proven by an Argument Made with Respect to the Signs of Love

It follows, therefore, to look at the argument made with respect to the signs of love, of which it suffices to discuss four for now.

Of these signs of love, the first is examination, as is said in the proverb: "where love is, there also are the eyes," certainly both the eyes of the body and of the mind. The part naturally examines the whole more than itself, as if it examines something more honest and more delightful and more useful to itself than it is on its own, as was discussed above.

The second is obedience, as is said in *John*: "He who loves me obeys my commandments."[244] The part must be more obedient to the whole than it is to itself, and the citizen must be more obedient to the law of the city than to his own desire, as if obeying a superior, who has greater jurisdiction; as if obeying something wiser, that which understands the truth more clearly; and as if obeying something better, that which wishes better things more effectively.

The third is work, or rather the tolerance for work, as is discussed in *Genesis* 29:20: "Jacob served for Rachel seven years and to him these seemed only few days because of the greatness of his love."[245] Bernard says as well: "My work seems like hardly an hour, and if it more than that, I do not feel it because of love;" Augustine too, in his work *On Sacred Widowhood*, says: "In him that which is loved either is not a labor or the labor itself is loved."[246] The cit-

---

[244] *John* 14:23.
[245] *Genesis* 29:20.
[246] Augustine *De sancta viduitate* c.21.

izen should labor more greatly for the community than for himself, and he must watch over it and die in battle for it etc..., as if for a greater advantage and glory and peace, just as is made clear from what was said above.

Fourth is the distribution of material goods, as is said in *The Song of Songs*: "If a man should offer the whole wealth of his household for love, it would be scorned as if it were nothing."[247] For this reason, indeed, the citizen must work more for his community than for himself, as there exists more benefit in the act of giving existence and other good things, and as there exists more generosity in giving. The citizen fails if he provides for himself alone, just as the hand does if it retains food for itself and does not provide it to the whole body, as is shows from what was said above.

These things are said to be signs and not proofs, just as good urine is said to be a sign of good health. Occasionally someone keeps watch over a person whom they hate in order to strike at them and does not keep watch over the person whom they should love more because of a moment of fault or in order to escape from evil. Similarly, occasionally someone obeys him whom he hates from fear or so that he may secretly cause him injury, since "he is unable to give injury, who shows that he wishes to do injury," as the saying attributed to Seneca goes; and does not obey him whom he loves because he asked the wrong way, so Tullius says in *On Friendship*: "Therefore this law is set forth in friendship, that we neither ask for shameful things, nor do them if asked."[248]

---

247 *The Song of Songs* 8:7.
248 Cicero *De Amicitia* c.12.

Similarly, occasionally someone works for him whom he hates for a similar reason to that one who obeys, and does not work for the one whom he loves for the same reason he does not keep watch over them. Similarly, occasionally gives to him whom he hates from fear, for instance to a tyrant; or from shame, for instance to some orphan; or from hope for some benefit or some thing that will be given in turn, for example to some prelate, or for some other reason; and does not give to him whom he loves because of the bad practices he serves, for example because he is a gambler or wasteful or visits brothels etc..., or because he wishes to conceal his love because of fear or for some other reason.

18: Arguments directed against the inquiry and their solutions.

Finally, those objections which seem to go against what has been discussed must be brought forward and each one explained. First, we shall discuss those arguments which are directed against the inquiry itself and following this will be those arguments which are seem to go against the examples that are given.

1. *The Counterargument*: the philosopher says in the ninth book of the *Nicomachaean Ethics* that the friendship we feel toward another arises from the friendship we feel toward ourselves.[249] Since the cause is always greater than the effect, in whatever matter, a human naturally loves himself more than anyone else.

---

[249] Aristotle *Nicomachean Ethics* IX. 1166a.

The Response. The whole is not another being or different from the part, rather the whole has a greater affinity to the part than there exists between the part and itself, as is made clear from the preceding discussions. The affinity which the whole has to the part is an actual affinity, while that which the part has for itself is a potential affinity only, since the part, inasmuch as it is a part, has no existence unless it is a potential existence, and, on the other hand, since the entire reason and cause for the existence of the part is the whole itself.

2. *The Counterargument.* Avicenna says that only God is generous in His action, since, for example, He does not pursue personal interests.[250] Therefore every creature loves his own personal interest first, since, as it seems, he pursues it naturally.

The Response. God alone can be said to be generous, just as is said in *Exodus*: "He is magnificent in holiness,"[251] since nothing can be added to Him from any other source, since He is the source of His own existence. Because of this, all creation is deficient and depends on others for its preservation and good. The part receives a greater completeness from the whole than from itself, just as is apparent from the previous discussion; from the whole it has its existence put in motion.

---

[250] Avicenna *Liber de Philosophia Prima* VI.5 and VIII.7.
[251] *Exodus* 15:11.

3. *The Counterargument.* According to Bernard of Clairveaux "human nature is bent back onto itself,"[252] therefore, any human naturally loves himself more than his community.

The Response. What Bernard says is true concerning corrupt nature and false love, for which reason, according to this truth, a human hates himself, just as it says in the *Psalms:* "He who loves iniquity hates his own soul;"[253] It is concerning this matter that the Apostle speaks when he says in second *Timothy:* "There will be men who love themselves, who are desirous, proud" etc...[254]

When considering incorrupt nature, that which Bernard says is partially true and partially not. It holds true in the case of passive action, but not in the case of active action. Fire is naturally moved upward for its conservation, but it does not act to create fire on its own account, but for the good of what is created, which is its form, and further on account of the common good, which is the conservation of the species; although its own conservation is even more disposed to the conservation of the whole, and not vice versa, otherwise there would be disorder in nature.

---

[252] Bernard of Clairveaux *Sermones super Cantica Canticorum* XXIV. 6-7.
[253] *Psalm* 10:6 (*Psalm* 11:5).
[254] II *Timothy* 3:2.

4. *The Counterargument:* According to the natural order everyone loves their own good; therefore, that which is a greater good is loved more. But the personal good of the part is greater for the part than the good of the whole is for the part. Therefore etc...

The Response: According to natural inclination, every person both loves their own personal good as well as the common good. But he loves the common good more than his personal good, just as is apparent from that which has been said.

5. *The Counterargument:* "The reason because of which something is so, is itself more so, as the reason because of which we love is loved more than the object of our love," as is said in the first book of the *Posterior Analytics.*[255] But the virtuous citizen, who exposes himself to death for the good of the city, would certainly not do such a thing unless he thought that doing this would bring him some advantage. No one does good unless on account of virtue; therefore he does this because of the good of virtue. The highest good of the citizen, then, is the good of virtue. Therefore etc...

The Response: Without doubt the good of the whole includes the good of the part. The primary purpose, however, is not first of all concerned with the part, since the good of the whole is a

---

[255] Aristotle *Posteriorum Analyticum* I.2: 72a 29-30.

greater good even for the part itself; just as a weight, moved up beyond the place where it exists properly, naturally must strive after the quiet of its proper place, it also strives to be moved downward, but not as its primary purpose; the movement is directed toward quiet and not the other way around.

Because of this, the good citizen does not expose himself to death because of the good of virtue, so to speak, because he is reaching for his primary purpose. This can be said, however, if the word "because" is used on account of the circumstances because of which the citizen is moved to do this work, just as if I were to say that fire heats "because" of heat or that the stone moves downward "because" of its weight.

But this same form of virtue, suppose that it can in some way be called the purpose, is futher directed to the more principal end, that is, to the object. This condition is revealed through the impulse and the impulse through the object, as is held in the second book of *On the Soul*,[256] that the impulse is the purpose of potential, and, as is held in the ninth book of the *Metaphysics*,[257] that the object is the purpose that is moved or that is moving due to the principal, if the impulse is of passive force. Therefore he speaks the truth, if he says "because"

---

[256] Aristotle *De Anima* II.4: 415a 16-28.
[257] Aristotle *Metaphysics* IX.8 1050a.

of inclusion or form or purpose, but not final purpose.

6. *The Counterargument.* Since that which is true and that which is good correspond, then just as that which is true holds itself to the truth, that which is good holds itself to the good. But that truth is the greatest truth which is a premise of itself, since, according to Boethius, "nothing is a more true premise than that in which the same is premised and concluded;"[258] and, according to the philosopher in the fifth book of the *Metaphysics,* the proposal "human is human" is true not only in itself but also because of the premise.[259] Therefore that good is the greatest good which is attributed each one to itself, i.e. the good of the part attributed to the part itself will be the greatest good. But since it is the greatest good it is also the most to be loved. Therefore etc...

The Response. The part can be looked at in two ways: first of all it can be treated as a thing in itself as it possesses a type of existence, on the other hand it can be treated as a part. The good which is naturally of the part, in its treatment as a part, is greater and more natural than that which is naturally of the part in its treatment as a thing in itself. The part is called such in respect to its whole, and therefore the good of the whole is for it the most natural and the most to be loved since the exist-

---

[258] Boethius *In Categorias Aristotelis Commentaria* VI.14.
[259] Aristotle *Metaphysics* V. 1022a.

ence of the part, in as much as it is a part, depends entirely on the whole.

7. *The Counterargument.* In as much as something is a greater good in itself, it does not necessarily follow that it is loved more greatly by nature, unless it is a greater good for the lover, otherwise water would naturally love fire more greatly than itself even though it naturally hates it. Similarly, in as much as something is the greater good of that which is loved it does not follow that it is loved more greatly by nature, unless it is personal good. So a human naturally loves more beneficiaries more greatly than more kinsmen, and occasionally more than himself, for example his master and suchlike.

Therefore, as much as the good of the whole is a greater than the good of the part in itself and is even the greater good for the part, it does not follow, however, because of this that the part naturally loves this good more since it is not, as it were, particular to the part as a good solely of the part would be, since the part is one thing and the whole another.

The Response. Certainly the good of the whole is not particular to the part as a good solely of the part would be, nevertheless it is naturally loved more by the part since the whole is the entire reason and cause for the existence of the part in as much as it is a part of the whole. Because of this we see that the part, having been separated from its own nature, naturally follows the nature of the whole, just as becomes apparent when water is moved upward lest a vacuum form, as was discussed above.

8. *The Counterargument*: God must be loved above all others according to the order of love, therefore also naturally, since grace does not destroy nature, but perfects it. God must be loved according to the order of love, however, because of the private good, as is seen in *Psalms*: "I always incline my heart to the doing of Your commandments for the reward."[260] Therefore the whole is loved by the part on account of the private good of the part.

The Response: Reward can be understood in two ways. The first way is to understand it objectively, and so the reward is God Himself, as God says to Abraham in *Genesis*: "I am your protector and your great reward."[261] The other way of understanding is participative, and so the reward pertains to desirous love; and because this cannot be an ultimate purpose, since desirous love is ordered toward the love of friendship as if to something better, but it is a purpose subordinate to a higher purpose. Just so we say that the just man, as if because of the final purpose, mainly does good, shuns the wickedness of sin and bears the ill of punishment for God, as is discussed in *Psalms*: "on your

---

[260] *Psalm* 119:112.
[261] *Genesis* 15:1.

account we are killed the whole day long, we are considered like sheep for the slaughter."[262]

Nevertheless, for the purposes of this argument we say that he who does these things cannot be separated from God and will not be punished with eternal damnation, as is said in *Psalms*: "let my heart be made immaculate in your commandments that I not be confounded,"[263] and in *first Corinthians*: "I punish my body and force it into slavery, so that I, while preaching to others, not be shown false."[264]

9. *The Counterarugment*. It is said in *Matthew*: "What does it serve a human if he acquires the entire world, while he suffers detriment to his soul?"[265] *Mark* and *Luke* have similar admonishments.[266] From these words can be seen that the good of one single soul is to be preferred over the good of the whole world.

The Response. The Lord is speaking of the profit of worldly things, as is seen in the *Glossa*: "in times of peace worldly desires are to be shattered;" and again he says: "neither profit nor fear nor anything else can return health."[267] Certainly the good

---

[262] *Psalm* 44:23.
[263] *Psalm* 119:80.
[264] *Corinthians* 9:27.
[265] *Matthew* 16:26.
[266] *Mark* 8:36 and *Luke* 9:25.
[267] *Glossa ordinaria a Matteo* 16:26 (Panella).

of the soul is to be preferred over every good of worldly profit.

If, however, the Lord were speaking of the profit of those who lead others to salvation, as that which a preacher is said to receive from men, turning them to repentance, as is said in first *Corinthians*: "I have made myself a servant of all, that I could profit many,"[268] and in the *Glossa*: "that is as having made profit of my preaching," if this were so, then it must be said that such profit of "the entire world" was made through the effort of some human, by word or by deed, and so cannot be in accordance with the true love of this human to the whole.

The love of the part for the whole includes the love it has for itself, and the good of the whole includes the good of the part, just as was made clear above. Therefore no human who has sinned in word or in deed, for example through hypocrisy, can love his community, since through sin he creates the true evil of his soul, and he hates himself with a true hatred, so is seen in *Psalms*: "He who works iniquity hates his own soul."[269]

10. *The Counterargument*: It says in *Exodus*: "you do not follow the multitude in wicked deeds."[270] Therefore anyone should wish that the communi-

---

[268] I *Corinthians* 9:19.
[269] *Psalm* 10:6.
[270] *Exodus* 23:2.

ty would sin rather than himself. But to be free from sin is a certain good, as the philosopher says in the fifth book of the *Nicomachaean Ethics*,[271] and, as he also says, to love something means to wish for its good. Therefore someone is not held to love the community more than himself.

The Response. The solution to this counterargument is to be understood in three ways. The first way is with regard to God, since following the order of love it is necessary to love God above all things. God is, however, offended by sin, and therefore no human ought to be driven to sin for any love whether for the community or otherwise. Therefore it is not the love of the individual that is being preferred to that of the community, but the love of God.

What's more, it is necessary that the love of the part is included in the love of the whole, as was stated above; and similarly the sin of the part is included in the sin of the whole of which it is a part, for this reason the part must flee the sins of the community more than its own. This is the solution to the argument using the subject.

That which is evil according to its nature can in no way be done with a good purpose, as both the philosopher and Augustine say; as sin is evil according to its nature. Therefore no one ought to sin, since

---

[271] Aristotle *Nicomachean Ethics* V. 1129b.

no love is so great that he should be defiled on its account. This is the solution to the argument using sin

11. *The Counterargument.* Any person is held to whish more, as we have seen, that his community be condemned to the inferno and not he, rather than that he be condemned and not the community, even if it is the whole world. But the evil of punishment [unlike that of sin] is directed against he who is suffering and not against God, who is, as Augustine says, the author of every punishment. Therefore a human is held not to love the community above himself.

The Response. Being punished with damnation presupposes fault in the person receiving the punishment which remains simultaneously with the punishment; thus it is, in fact, an offense to God, whom we must love above the whole world, and because of this love for God to rejoice in the punishment, even that of hell, meted out to whatever community by God because of the offense given to God, as is said in *Psalms:* "the just man rejoices when he sees vengeance."[272]

If, however, it would be possible for punishment to exist without the precondition of sin, then the man must, because of the power of the order of love, wish more to suffer himself, since he is a part

---

[272] *Psalm* 57:11.

of the community, if the community would be immune, than that his own community suffer, if he would be immune.

12. *The Counterargument.* Augustine says in the first book of his *On Christian Doctrine:* "four things exist which must be loved: first of all that which is above us – that is to say God--, the second is ourselves, third is that which is joined to us – that is our neighbor --, the fourth is that which is below us"[273] that is our body, since happiness flows over and down onto it. But among these four levels the community cannot be found, unless it pertains to the neighbor, whom without doubt we should love after ourselves.

The Response. The community, on the one hand, pertains both to us and to our neighbor, in as much as both we and our neighbor are parts of it. On the other hand, it pertains to God as well, in as much as God is the common and complete good for all, and for this reason, just as God is naturally more loved by all things, since He is the cause of being and beauty for all things, so, after God, the whole should be loved more by the part in as much as it is the reason for the existence and the beauty of the part. The philosopher did well in the first book of the *Nicomachaean Ethics* where he joins the love of the community with God, saying that it

---

[273] Augustine *De doctrina Christiana* I.23 6-8.

is better and more divine to love the community than it is to love a single person alone.[274]

13. *The Counterargument.* The love of the individual is of no worth unless it is directed toward a rational thing; but the community in itself is not rational, therefore etc...

The Response. The community should not be hereunderstood according to the entirety of the universal whole, but of an integral whole, therefore not exactly and principally from a corporeal part but from a rational part. Therefore it is loved exactly because of this rationality; it is also loved more, following God, because of the similarity it shares with God, who is certainly the highest form of rationality.

14. *The Counterargument.* When something touches on the whole reason of the part,[275] it has touched the part more than the whole since that which originates is always stronger. For example, being snub-nosed touches more upon the nose than the whole person, since it is the personal defect of the nose and not of the whole person. Similarly one could speak of curls in the hair or a curve in the back. The community, however, is not loved directly in the order of love unless because of the reason of its parts, in which, just as in its individu-

---

[274] Aristotle *Nicomachean Ethics* I. 1094b.
[275] i.e. ratio.

al subject, is love. Therefore any citizen is loved more than the city according to the order of love.

The Response. For the present, reason can be discussed in two ways: reason that is material and less original and reason that is formal and more original (that is to say reason without which something cannot exist, and reason because of which something exists). For example, the material reason without which color cannot be seen is the body; the truly formal reason because of which color can be seen is light.

The material reason without which nothing is able to be directly loved according to the order of love, is rational or intellectual existence; but the formal reason because of which something is loved, that is God Himself. Whatever things, then, that we love, we must love them because of God, who allows the inflowing of love and is its ultimate and principal goal. Since the totality of rational creatures is considered more by God than any one specific part of it, any part of this totality must, then, love it more, after God, than any other part of this totality or even itself.

15. *The Counterargument.* A boy naturally loves his mother more than his fatherland.

The Response. A boy, in as much as he is a specific individual and existing, as it were, as a specific whole, loves his mother naturally more than his fatherland, as if more closely joined to her. While

Porfirius says that: "the fatherland is the origin of every generation, in the same way as a father,"[276] nevertheless, the father is the intrinsic origin and has a closer relationship than the others of the fatherland. Inasmuch as the boy is a part of the fatherland, however, he ought to love it more, unless he is impeded by the stain of original sin: since love is felt for only that which is known. Therefore a distinction must be made between the part of the boy, the part of understanding and the part of nature, whole or corrupt.

16. *The Counterargument:* According to the law God must be loved above all things, parents second of all and third of all the fatherland. Therefore one ought to love oneself more than the fatherland.

The Response: The laws are understood to speak of a man loving considered as a specific whole, existing on his own and not as a part of the fatherland. So the whole fatherland is understood as being closer than the neighbor. Amongst neighbors the one who is closest must be loved the most.

17. *The Counterargument:* Christ, whose nature was without any sin, loved Himself more than the whole race of man, because of natural desire, as is said in *Matthew:* "Father, if it possible, let this cup pass from me; but not, however, as I will, but as You will."[277]

---

[276] Porfirius *Isagoge* II.4.
[277] *Matthew* 26:39.

The Response. Nothing exists in Christ unless it is a rational desire, which is also a natural desire, since the rational desire was a certain natural power of his soul. Nevertheless occasionally voluntary action is divided against natural action, in as much as nature is limited to one, not, however, desire. Therefore desire too is distinguished in its action since it can be understood as nature, and so be carried into something in an absolute sense, and so Christ would not wish to die, since every death is contrary to nature; but it can be accepted as desire, and so he is brought to this point for others, and so Christ wishes for death for the salvation of the human race, as is said in *Isaiah:* "He is offered according to His wish."[278] First is incomplete desire and second is a complete and absolute desire.

18. The Counterargument. According to the order of love, one must love charity more in oneself than in the whole rest of the world, and the same is true for happiness.

The Response. In this matter a dual distinction must be made: one distinction comes from the subject, that is the person who is loved and the other from the principal object, which is God.

First of all, since the subject can be considered a certain whole or, like the part of the multitude of

---

[278] *Isaiah* 53:7.

the city is, ecclesiastically, militant or triumphant, in this first case the counterargument holds, since the whole other multitude of creatures is considered as a neighbor.

In the second case it does not hold, since, just like the part, in as much as it is a part, has no existence unless it comes from the whole, so it can have neither charity nor happiness nor any other thing which necessarily presuppose existence. For this reason that which Moses said in *Exodus* and the Apostle in *Romans* can be set forth, as was said above.[279] Because of this *Ephesians* says: "Already you are not guests or strangers, but citizens of the holy and servants of God."[280] *Glossa*: "each person asks himself whom he should love and he will find whence he is a citizen."

Following, then, the order of love one is to love God first; second the city of God, whether militant or triumphant, as is said in *Psalms*: "glorious things are said of you, city of God;"[281] third himself; fourth any fellow citizen *in se*.

The second distinction is that God can be considered the immediate cause of all love, of all happiness and all spiritual and natural existence; so is said in *Ezekiel*: "all souls are mine."[282] This is seen

---

[279] *Exodus* 23 and *Romans* 9.
[280] *Ephesians* 2:19.
[281] *Psalm* 86:3.
[282] *Ezekiel* 18:41.

most in spiritual creatures, which exist throughout creation. So the love by which someone loves himself is seen as the love of God, as the original and immediate causal principal, because of which one loves himself: "it is just for all things to be named for their cause" as is said in the second book of the work *On the Soul*.[283] It can be looked at in another way as well, understood as the principle of the order of love, that is to say, as it is moved from whole to a part. And this, then, comes out to the same thing.

Or, said a better way. The solution can be understood two ways. In the first way this can be understood in relationship to God, who is loved first and blessed first; and so everything else must be loved in accordance with its order toward Him. Because of this the love and happiness of God is to be preferred and following this the love and happiness of the whole, not the love or happiness of the self. The second way this can be understood is in relationship to the subject, which was discussed above, in as much as it is a certain individual *in se* etc...; and so blessed Augustine restored the community to its place among those things which count as a neighbor in his list of four when he says "four things exist which must be loved according to the order of love,"[284] or said another way, since a part comes from a certain whole; and so Augustine un-

---

[283] Aristotle *De Anima* II.4: 416b 23-24.
[284] Augustine *De Doctrina Christiana* I.23 6-9.

derstands the community among those things which we are ourselves.

The Counterargument. A human is not able not to strive for his own happiness because of natural love, and nevertheless he can strive that it exists for no one else in the community.

The Response. He cannot do so in as much as he is a part of the community, since he would then not be striving for his own.

19. Arguments against the given examples concerning the object, and their solutions.

We will discuss, of course, those arguments which seem to run contrary to those examples that have been given, and first of all those which deal with the object.

1. *The Counterargument.* The common ill has more in common with the common good, as it pertains to the community, than the individual good; but nevertheless, evil is in no way to be loved.

   The Response. Mere commonality of object does not suffice for love, unless there exists as well a similar excellence. The common good unites both sides in harmony.

2. *The Counterargument.* Occasionally my neighbor is better, nevertheless, I am not held to love him ahead of myself, but after myself.

   The Response. The whole is itself the better part, since from it depends the total goodness of each individual part, which is not dependant on the goodness of a neighbor who is better.

3. *The Counterargument*: The good solitary life is to be preferred over the public life, just as we laid out in a number of places in the treatise *Against the False Teachers of the Church*.[285] But the solitary life is focused on the love of self, the public life, however, on the love of the community. Therefore etc.

The Response: The virtuous solitary man is not to be assessed by man, but by God, this follows the philosopher both in the tenth book of the *Nicomachean Ethics* and in the first book of the *Politics*.[286] Therefore in this type of life the love of a single person is not preferred over the love of the community, but the love of God is preferred over the love of any part of creation.

20. Arguments against the given examples concerning the subject, and their solutions.

Objections to the subject are given thus:

The Counterargument: A greater affinity exists where there is no inner difference than where some such difference exists. There exists no inner difference between the part and itself, neither in name nor in matter. The whole, however, assuredly differs from the part not only in name, since there exists one name for

---

[285] Here Remigius dei Girolami references another of his own works, the *Contra Falsos Ecclesie Professores*.

[286] Aristotle *Nicomachean Ethics* X. 1177b and Aristotle *Physics* I.2: 1253a 27-29.

the part and a different name for the whole, but in matter as well. Not only are the part and the whole different according to their name, even when they mean the same thing, so it is with "Tullius" and "Cicero" and with "longsword" and "broadsword;" but this pertains to the different type of relationship, since the whole inhabits the superposition and the part the subposition. Therefore the affinity of the part to itself is greater than that of the part to the whole.

The Response: The affinity in name alone is insufficient to create a true affinity; the differences between the dog star and the barking dog, which have an affinity according to the name of their type, as both are certainly called "dog," are truly greater than those between the barking dog and the braying donkey, whose species have different names.

Matter is twofold, there exists, for example, matter itself, that is existing itself, and there is matter that is potential, that exists by the power of the agent, agent being, broadly understood, any means by which something is influenced. Therefore it must be said that the existing matter should certainly have a greater affinity to itself than the agent to the existing matter. Nevertheless the agent is more closely joined to that potential matter, since it does not have the virtue of existence from itself, but through the influence of the agent. Therefore we say, following that saying attributed to blessed Augustine, that "God is closer to whatever creature than it is to itself," since the power that sustains it does not derive from itself, but from God; this example is as if we said that the figure on a sigil is closer to a figure impressed in water than that figure is to itself since without the presence of the sigil it would not exist for even a moment.

For this reason we say that the principal agent is more immediately effective than the instrumental agent, since "every primary cause affects more than a secondary cause," as is said in the first proposition of the book *On Causes*.[287] We say therefore that the vicar labors as mediator to the bishop, the steward as mediator to the king and the servant as mediator to the master.

For this reason we also say that the whole has a greater affinity to the part than the part to itself, although the opposite is the supposition. But since the first affinity is greater than the second, just as the origin is greater than that which is created, therefore simply it must be said that the whole has simply more affinity to the part than the part to itself and certainly, following this, the opposite is true as well.

21. Arguments against the given examples concerning the causes, and their solutions.

The examples given for the causes of love are given thus.

1. *The Counterargument:* We know our neighbor more than God, and we are aware of the creature before the Creator; nevertheless according to the order of love we must love God above all things.

---

[287] Ps. Aristotle *De Causis* I.

The Response. Prior knowledge alone or even greater knowledge does not suffice for something to be loved more by something else according to the natural order, although this is certainly a possiblity, but it is necessary that simultaneously with the prior or greater knowledge there should also be a greater good in itself and a good even more joined to the loved one.

2. *The Counterargument.* The love by which someone loves someone else personally, is the love of desire. But the love of friendship is greater than the love of desire. If, therefore, the part loves the whole more than itself for this reason, that the whole is a greater good for it than it is for itself, then it loves itself with the love of friendship, which certainly leads someone to wish good for that which it loves, it follows then that the love by which it loves itself according to nature is stronger than that love by which it naturally loves the whole.

The Response. The part naturally loves the whole with the love of friendship. But because even the good of the lover is included in the good of the beloved, it is said that the part loves the whole because of its personal good; not because the good of the whole is turned to the individual good, but because the individual good is attuned to the good of the whole.

3. *The Counterargument.* The similarity we have with our neighbor, with whom we have our type

in common, is greater than the similarity we have with God, with whom we only have existence in common, since God is beyond all type. But we believe from the natural order of love, that we must lover God more than our neighbor. Therefore the greater similarity of the part to the whole is insufficient cause for it to love the whole more than itself.

The Response. The similarity which we have with God is not through some participation with Him, nor even through common existence, but it is through imitation, just like, for example, a work is made similar to the artificer; and is therefore stronger than the similarity we have to our neighbor, which is through a type of participation with him, just as the cause is greater than the effect. The similarity with our neighbor also arises from the fact that both participate in God, and that which is from Him our neighbor possesses also, and so a likeness is created; and for this reason of similarity we must love God more than our neighbor.

The arguments against the examples with respect to the effects and signs of love are various. But nevertheless, whatever should have been said differently before in order to explain the truth more readily or to be more persuasive – for instance by putting the arguments first and then the examples, or first the arguments and then the counter-arguments, or using some other order—the diligent reader should discern this and adjust the text accordingly.

Here ends the treatise concerning the good of the community by Brother Remigius of Florence, a teacher of theology of the Dominican order.

Texts Cited in the *De Bono Communi*

I. Classical References.

Artistotle *De Anima* – 72; 81; 101; 111

Aristotle *Nicomachean Ethics* – 55; 70; 72; 73; 75; 82; 83; 84; 85; 87; 89; 91; 92; 105; 107

Aristotle *Physics* – 57; 72; 79; 89; 92; 113

Aristotle *Politics* – 72; 73; 91

Aristotle *Posteriorum Analyticum* – 80; 101

Aristotle *Predicamentorum* – 80

Aristotle *Metaphysics* – 72; 80; 102

Aristotle *Rethoricae* – 92

Aristotle *Topicorum* – 55; 81

Ps. Aristotle *De Causis* – 115

Boethius *In Categorias Aristotelis Commentaria* – 102

Cicero *De Amicitia* – 97

Cicero *De Natura Deorum* – 82

Cicero *De Oficiis* – 56

Cicero *Oratio in Catilinam Prima in Senatu Habita* – 56

Cicero *Pro Ligario* -- 55

Ps. Cicero *Ivectia contra Salustium* – 56

Ps. Cicero *Oratione Populari ad Senatum* – 56

Dionysius Cato *Monasticha Catonis* – 56

Ovid *Epistulae Ex Ponto* – 76; 82

Phaedrus Augustus-Libertus *Fabulae Aesopiae* – 60

Plutarch *Vita Catonis* – 63

Porfirius *Isagoge* – 109

Ps. Dionysius the Areopagyte *De Divinis Nominibus* – 70; 74

Ps. Seneca *De Remediis Fortuitorum* – 87

Valerius Maximus *Factorum ac Dictorum Memorabilium* – 61; 62; 64

II. Old Testamen References

Genesis – 96; 103

III. New Testament References

IV. Patristic References

Augustine *De Civitate Dei* – 60; 61; 64

Augustine *De Doctrina Christiana* – 107; 112

Augustine *De Libero Arbitrio* – 72; 93

Augustine *De Origine Animae* – 58

Augustine *De Sancta Viduitate* – 96

Augustine *De Trinitate* – 79; 91

Augustine *Enchiridion* – 71

Augustine *Epistulae* – 83

Augustine *Regula* – 54; 75

V. Other References

Avicenna *Liber de Philosophia Prima* – 99

Bernard of Clairveaux *Sermones super Cantica Canticorum* – 100

Petrus Comestor *Historia Scholastica* – 65

Remigius Dei Girolami *Contra Falsos Ecclesie Professores* – 113

Remigius Dei Girolami *De Modis Rerum* – 81

The De Bono Pacis

Introduction to the *De Bono Pacis*[288]

Where the *De Bono Communi* lays out a generalized argument for citizens to prefer the common good over their own good, the *De Bono Pacis* explores one of the consequences that the various wrongs committed against each other by the Guelfs, Ghibellines, and other factions in the city. It is these wrongs that need to be forgiven for the dissolution of the state to be healed, and for there to be peace in the city, which furthers the common good.[289]

The argumentation of Remigius's position here, mirrors that seen in the *De Bono Communi*, in that he centrally focuses on the relationship of the part to the whole. There are even many of the examples and analogies made by Remigius which are common to both texts.[290]

Stylistically, however, there are some major differences in how Remigius lays out the two texts. The *De Bono Pacis* is divided into two sections, in which, the premise is approached. The first discusses examples of "authority" which support the idea that ills must be forgiven for the good of peace, and that goods can be confiscated for the same purpose. The second section presents logical arguments that lead to the same conclusion. In this second section, Remigius seems to mimic the style of Thomas Aquinas in the *Summa Theologica* much more closely. Including, counterarguments and their solutions in each section, before making his own argument.

The relationship between the *De Bono Pacis* and the *De Bono Communi*, both in focus and in style of argu-

---

[288] The Latin text I used for this translation is from the edition in Panella (2014), 222-247. This edition also contains copious notes and a translation into Italian.

[289] For an in-depth discussion see Panella (2014), 19-36.

[290] Discussed in the individual sections below.

mentation, beg the question: which treatise was written earlier?[291] An attempt at dating the texts has been made by Emilio Panella who is able to place the *De Bono Communi*. The description of the state of Florence made in the *De Bono Communi* finds congruence only in the devastation which followed the return of the banished black Guelfs and of Corso dei Donati on the 5th of November 1301. "The *De Bono Communi* must, then, come after this date."[292] The comparative dating of the two texts is a bit more complicated. Panella does, however, discuss the possibility that the *De Bono Communi* was written prior to the *De Bono Pacis*. "Less preemptory is the priority of the *De Bono Communi* in respect to the *Bono Pacis*; but in our own judgment the textual comparison of the two treatises offers remarkable evidence to consider that the *De Bono Communi* served in the composition of the *De Bono Pacis* and is therefore earlier."[293] In section I of the *De Bono Pacis*, he discusses passages of Scripture from Aristotle, Augustine, and Cicero, which were discussed in more detail in sections I, II and V of the *De Bono Communi*. In section III of the *De Bono Pacis*, Remigius dei Girolami again discusses texts, mostly from Aristotle, in the context of the part and the whole, which he discussed in section IX of the *De Bono Communi*. While the textual corre-

---

[291] Panella (2014), 36.

[292] Panella (2014), 38-57. "La descrizione dello stato di Firenze fatta nel De bono comuni trova congruo riscontro soltanto nella devastazione che seguì il rientro degli sbanditi neri e di Corso dei Donati il 5 novembre 1301. Il De bono comuni va pertanto collocato a ridosso di quest'ultima data."

[293] Ibid. "Meno perentoria è la priorità del *De bono comuni* rispetto al *De bono pacis*; ma a nostro giudizio il raffronto testuale dei due trattati offre evidenze di notevole peso per ritenere che il *De bono comuni* abbia servito la composizione del *De bono pacis* e sia pertanto ad esso anteriore."

lations are not necessarily telling, Remigius could just as easily take ideas developed in the *De Bono Pacis* and expound on them in more detail in the *De Bono Communi*. One indication that the *De Bono Pacis* may, in fact, be the earlier text is the even more obvious dependence of the *De Bono Pacis* on Thomas Aquinas' *Summa Theologica* in layout. In the *De Bono Pacis* each section is laid out with counterarguments and their resolution following a short introduction.

While the counterarguments and resolutions are only found at the end of the whole argument in the *De Bono Communi* (starting in section XVIII). It is the logical progression of thought from the *De Bono Communi* to the *De Bono Pacis*, that is, perhaps, most convincing in this discussion. The progression from the theoretical foundation for building peace in a commune riven by dissent, the understanding that the citizen exists as part of the whole and must work for the good of the whole, rather than their own good, to a more practical justification, that for this peace it is proper to force forgiveness between parties, even though the confiscation and redistribution of their goods.

Arguments from Authority

The first set of argumentations Remigius gives for his premise is made in section one of the *De Bono Communi* and come from a variety of sources of "authority:" 1. philosophy, 2. sacred Scripture, 3. the saints, 4. canon law and 5. civil law. This section is especially interesting in the discussion of the relationship between the *De Bono Pacis* and the *De Bono Communi* as the examples given from philosophy, sacred Scripture, and the saints correspond to the examples given in the first two sections of the *De Bo-*

no Communi. If, as Panella argues, the *De Bono Communi* is the earlier work, then these arguments from authority are a summary of those given in the *De Bono Communi.* The argumentation in the *De Bono Communi* seems, however, an expanded, more well developed, argument. This, again, suggests that the *De Bono Pacis* may have been the earlier work and provided source material for the *De Bono Communi.* One aspect of the *De Bono Pacis* that sets it apart from the *De Bono Communi* is a much heavier reliance on legal documents. Applying both canon and civil law to the question, a focus which is seen again in the *De Iustiti.*

Logical Argumentation

The basic premise of the *De Bono Pacis* is that peace is the highest good, and that in reaching the good of peace, "wrongs and injuries that have been done to us can be forgiven and if we can receive the same from other communities… without the assent of each individual person of those cities or communities, or even more against the will of any of those persons who have suffered wrongs and injuries." This is a rather radical notion, that whatever wrong was committed, it must be put aside for the good of peace. This notion is closely related to that which drives the *De Bono Communi.* The factions within the city of Florence, and Italy in general must reach a peaceful resolution, but the texts approach this from two different angles. Where the *De Bono Communi* offers a general plea to put the good of the community over the infighting, the *De Bono Pacis* confronts the issue of how this is to be done. This difference in focus is, perhaps, the best evidence for the *De Bono Pacis* being secondary, continuing the discussion of the *De Bono Communi.*

Following the initial discussion of arguments coming from authority, the rest of the text is focused on proving this from a variety of perspectives: 1. God, 2. the world, 3. humans, 4. the Catholic Church, 5. purpose and 6. the ruler.

The De Bono Pacis

by Brother Remigius dei Girolami O.P.

It has been asked whether, for the good of peace and for the concord between cities and castles and other communities, wrongs and injuries that have been done to us can be forgiven and if we can receive the same from other communities, for the sake of unity among them all. It has also been asked whether this can be done without the assent of each individual person of those cities or communities, or even more against the will of any of those persons who have suffered wrongs and injuries, even those affiliated with the church.

It seems that this can answered in the affirmative, especially since it seems possible to prove this both with examples coming from authority as well as with examples arising from logic.

Arguments Coming from Authority

This idea can be proven by a multiplicity of authorities, for example by philosophy, Sacred Scripture, by the saints, by the canons of the church and by civil law.

1.1. As for the first of these authorities, philosophy, note that the Philosopher says in the first book of the *Nicomachaean Ethics* that the good of a people, of a city and of a multitude is to be preferred over the good of a single individual, since it is more divine and better.[294] The highest good of a multitude, however, and its purpose, is peace, as the philosopher says in the third book of the *Nicomachaean Ethics*,[295] just like, as he also says, health is the highest good of the body as a whole. For this reason, just like the good of one limb, which might even be cut off, is neglected for the health of the entire body,[296] so the good of one particular person must be neglected for the peace of the state.

Tullius says the same thing in the *Invective against Salust:* "However much someone supports the affairs of the Republic, so much is he my friend or my enemy."[297] In book one of the *On Moral Duties* he says: "They who are dedicated to the affairs of the Republic should hold ont to two precepts of Plato: the first is that they should watch over what is to the advantage of the citizenry, so that whoever should agitate, they would inform on him as sullying their own advantage; the other is that they do not take care of the entire body of the state until they watch

---

[294] Aristotle *Nicomachean Ethics* I. 1094b cf. Remigius dei Girolami *De Bono Communi* II.

[295] Aristotle *Nicomachean Ethics* III. 1112b.

[296] Cf. Remigius dei Girolami *De Bono Communi* V.

[297] Ps. Cicero *Invecta contra Salustium* IV. 11. Cf. Remigius dei Girolami *De Bono Communi* II.

over some part that the rest have forsaken."[298] Again he says in his *Invectives*: "The fatherland is far more dear to me than my life."[299]

1.2. As to the second source of authority, sacred Scripture. It is said of Onias, the high priest and perfect man in the second book of the *Maccabees* that: "he went to the king not as an accuser of the citizenry, but for the common good, considering the whole multitude in his own mind, for he saw that, without the providence of the king, it would be impossible to bring peace to the state and to hold back Simon from his folly."[300] Likewise in *John* Caiaphas himself, whom blessed John gives prophetic words, says that: "it is better for you that one man should die for the people than that the whole people should be destroyed."[301]

1.3. As to the third source of authority, the saints. Blessed Augustine expounding on first *Corinthians*, which says: "love does not search out those things which belong to it,"[302] in his *Rules* says: "love puts the community interests before its own;"[303] and again, later, he says: "however much more you care about the common good than about your own, so much more will you learn to advance." Similarly he says in the nineteenth book of the *City of God*: "so great is the good of peace that among all earthly and mortal things nothing is heard with greater

---

[298] Cicero *De Oficiis* I.16. Cf. Remigius dei Girolami *De Bono Communi* II.

[299] Cicero *Oratio in Catilinam Prima in Senatu Habita* I.11. Cf. Remigius dei Girolami *De Bono Communi* II.

[300] II *Maccabees* 4:4-6. Cf. Remigius dei Girolami *De Bono Communi* I.

[301] *John* 11:50. Cf. Remigius dei Girolami *De Bono Communi* I.

[302] I *Corinthians* 13:5.

[303] Augustine *Regula* Caput V.31. Cf. Remigus dei Girolami *De Bono Communi* I.

pleasure nothing longed for with greater desire, and finally, there exists nothing better that can be entered into."[304]

1.4. As to the fourth source of authority, canon law. It is said in canon 23 question 1, which begins *Nolite* and which deals with Augustine's *Letter to Boniface*: "be more peaceful in waging war, so that you may lead those, whom you have defeated, to the advantage of peace."[305] Similarly, the final question of canon 23, which begins *Tributum*, says: "it is necessary to pay the emperor from the material goods of the church, as is the ancient custom, for peace and quiet, for which they should watch over and defend us."[306]

Likewise in the *Extravagantes* the section which discusses *De emunitate ecclesiarum*, which begins *Pervenit*, says: "it should be suffered for no one to be excused from watching upon the walls, not in our name, or the name of his church, nor for any other reason; but all men are compelled to this, how much more everyone is vigilant, so much more secure is the state."[307] *Glossa*: "Since it is right for the state to have many defenders." The same is seen in the *Extravagantes* in the section which discusses *De iniuriis et dampno dato*, which begins *In nostra*, here it is said that: "for the good of peace he contributes to the repayment of expenses."[308] *Glossa*: "equal contribution is to be made for the good of peace and tranquility, lest by chance tranquility not be maintained because of this."

---

[304] Augustine *De Civitate Dei* XIX. 11.
[305] *Decretum Gratiani* Causa XXIII Quaestio I Canon III.
[306] *Decretum Gratiani* Causa XIII Quaestio VIII Canon XXII.
[307] *Liber Extravagantes* Liber III Titulum XLIX Capitulum II.
[308] *Liber Extravagantes* Liber V Titulum XXXVI Capitulum VIII.

1.5. As to the fifth source of authority, civil law. It suffices to say that civil laws permit many things, even evil ones, that is to say they do not punish them for the good of the community's peace, so for example usury and prostitution.

In proving this point through logic, arguments can be made with respect to six different points of view: first of all from the point of God.

The good of God is preferred over the good of any one of His creatures. Peace, however, is the good of God and pertains to God; like temporal things are a good pertaining to humans. Therefore, in striving for the good of peace, one must be prepared to endure injuries in temporal matters.

The lesser proposition is proven in all three members of the Trinity. The person of the Father begets the person of the Son, who Himself is the peace of humans, as is said in *Ephesians:* "He is our peace, who made two into one."[309] The person of the Son together with the person of the Father breathe forth the person of the Holy Spirit, who, breathed forth by both, is the peace and concord of both, as is said by Augustine in book one of his *On Christian Doctrine:* "in the Father is unity, in the Son is equality, in the Holy Spirit is concord, that is unity and equality; all these three are one on account of the Father, are equal because of the Son and are connected because of the Holy Spirit."[310] In the eighth book of *On the Trinity* he says:

---

[309] *Ephesians* 2:14.
[310] Augustine *De Doctrina Christiana* I.5 15-18.

"the Holy Spirit is the highest love, joining the two and subjoining us,"[311] that is joining us together under God.

The Counterargument: Since it is said of God the Father in *Jeremiah:* "I have brought my peace to the people, says the Lord."[312] "The Lord is the name of power," as Abrosius said in book one of *On the Trinity;* power is, in fact, appropriated by God the Father.[313] The Son says in *Matthew:* "I have come to bring not peace, but the sword."[314] Of the Holy Spirit is said by *Isaiah:* "like a violent flood, whom the Spirit of the Lord summons."[315]

The Response: Peace can be understood properly and truly; and so it is included in good, as order is as well, since peace includes order in it, as Augustine says in book nineteen of *The City of God.*[316] So *Isaiah* 59 says as well: "there is no peace for the impious, says the Lord."[317] Or it can be understood metaphorically, like the saying "the perfect robber," as is said in the fifth book of the *Metaphysics,* or more clearly, as is said in *The Wisdom of Solomon:* "living in a great ignorant war, and they call such a great evil peace."[318]

Waging war (the opposite of peace) has two possible purposes: the first is war as a purpose in itself, the second is as a way to create peace, since occasionally through war it is possible to come to peace, just as is made clear by the philosopher in the ninth book of the *Nicomachaean Eth-*

---

[311] Augustine *De Trinitate* VIII.3 85-86.

[312] *Jeremiah* 16:5.

[313] Ambrosius *De Trinitate* Caput I (PL XVII columns 537-539). Panella suggests Ambrosius *De Fide* I (PL XVI column 30).

[314] *Matthew* 10:34.

[315] *Isaiah* 59:19.

[316] Augustine *De Civitate Dei* XIX. 13.

[317] Panella points out that *Isaiah* 48:22 is meant.

[318] *The Wisdom of Solomon* 14:22.

ics and by Augustine in the nineteenth book of the *City of God.*[319]

The removal of peace occurs in two ways: one way is causative, the other permissive. God takes away good peace from sinners permissively, allowing them to fall into wicked peace. Or he does this punitively, on account of the good of true peace.

God removes good peace from sinners through crimes and desires, or at the hand of humans and demons because of their crimes; the Holy Spirit makes certain violence, according to what was said above, for example against the appetites of the flesh, as is said in *Matthew*: "the kingdom of the heavens has suffered violence and those who are violent have sacked it."[320]

The Counterargument: The Lord said in *Luke*: "those who hear you, hear me."[321] But the prelates of the church prohibit these things discussed above on account of peace or some other good. Therefore God prohibits this.

The Response: These words of the Lord must be understood to hold true when the prelates of the church are in agreement with Christ, most of all in their intentions. This is like one who, hearing a messenger hears the lord who sent him, and, hearing a steward, hears the true master, when the messenger and the steward are in agreement with the lord and the master. When, however they are not in agreement with him they do not hear the lord. In this case, if the lord is just, it is unnecessary for them

---

[319] Aristotle *Nicomachean Ethics* X 1175b (Panella) and Augustine *De Civitate Dei* XIX.12 1-14.
[320] *Matthew* 11:12.
[321] *Luke* 10:6.

to be heard, as is said in *The Acts of the Apostles*: "it is better to obey the Lord more than humans."[322]

Arguments coming from the consideration of the world.

The good of the world consists of peace, that is in the tranquility of its parts toward one another; just as Augustine says in book nineteen of *The City of God*: "the peace of the body is the ordered temperance of the parts,"[323] and "the peace of all things is the tranquility of order."[324] It is in this order that the good of the world rests, according to the philosopher in the twelfth book of the *Metaphysics*, where he says that: "all things are somehow coordinate."[325] But the good of the whole is preferred over the good of the part. Therefore, the good of peace must be preferred over the earthly good of particular persons.

The Counterargument: Injury is to be done to no one, nor is the evil of punishment to be inflicted on someone without a crime, for the greater good; nor is it proper to confiscate the possessions of a sinful man, or even a man who is merely less good, that they should be given to a just man who would use them better. Therefore, it is not allowed for a person to be deprived of his possessions without his consent for the greater good of the whole community, which is said to be peace. He is even robbed by them, if they do not restore those things to him or restitution given to him.

The Response: It must be said that, according to the truth, such a removal of belongings should not be understood as an injustice nor as punitive, however much it be

---

[322] *The Acts of the Apostles* 5:29.
[323] Augustine *De Civitate Dei* XIX.13.
[324] Ibid.
[325] Aristotle *Metaphysics* XII.10 1075a 11-17.

done against the will of the owner since many benefits are given to reluctant people. Augustine puts many examples of this in his *Letter to Vincentius the Donatist*.[326] This is discussed as well in canon 23 question 5, which begins *Nimium*, that a madman is restrained against his will, lest he throws himself headlong and that a boy is chastened with rods.[327]

Such a confiscation of belongings, which is done for peace, the good of the community, is a greater good for the particular person than if the goods were not taken from him. This is so, since the good of the whole is the greater good of the part, in as much as it is a part, than the good of the part is for itself. The existence of the part, in as much as it is a part and all the goods which are the consequence of existence, depend on the existence and good of the whole, as.

The part, beyond the existence of the whole, is not a part, as it is said to be while it exists as part of the whole. A hand which is cut off is not a hand anymore, except ambiguously, as one would about a hand that is made of stone, or painted, as is made clear by the philosopher in the second book of the *On the Soul* and in the seventh book of the *Metaphysics* and in the first book of the *Politics*.[328] Such a hand no longer operates as a hand, it cannot sense the things it touches, it cannot bring food to the mouth, it cannot scratch nor do other such things, because of this the philosopher says in the first book of the

---

[326] Augustine *Ad Vincentium Donatistam* passim.

[327] *Decretum Gratiani* Causa XXIII Quaestio IV Canon XXXVII.

[328] Aristotle *De Anima* II.1 412b 20-22; Aristotle *Metaphysics* VII.10 1035b 24-25; Aristotle *Politics* I.2 1253a 20-21. Cf. Remigius dei Girolami *De Bono Communi* IX.

Politics: "a city is set before a house and before each of us individually; for the whole is necessarily set before the part. For should the whole be destroyed there will be neither foot nor hand, except ambiguously, like someone would discuss one made of stone; such a thing will be destroyed. All things are defined by their function and virtue; for this reason, if they no longer serve this function they can in no way be called this except ambiguously,"[329] since they lack the operation and virtue by which they are defined, since the definition of "foot" is an organic member which has the virtue of walking.

Therefore in the destruction of the state, which occurs in the dissension of the citizens, since the city is said to be the unity of its citizens, as is said by Isidore in book fifteen of the *Etymologies*,[330] the citizen remains as if stone or painted, since he certainly lacks the operation and virtue which he had before: the soldier in military matters, the merchant in selling, the artist in the carrying out of his art, the official in his office, the head of the family in family affairs and the universally free man in his freedom, that is in going to visit his holdings, in making embassies, in having dominion over foreign cities and suchlike.[331]

The fourth argument is made with respect to humans.

A human is naturally inclined to creating a community with another, or with others either in cities or in castles and so forth; after all, he is a creature that is by na-

---

[329] Aristotle *Politics* I.2 1253a 19-24. Cf. Remigius dei Girolami *De Bono Communi* IX.

[330] Isidore *Etymologiae* XV.2.

[331] Cf. Remigius dei Girolami *De Bono Communi* IX.

ture communal and political, as the philosopher says in the eighth book of the *Nicomachaean Ethics* and in the first book of the *Politics*.[332] This community is focused on peace, while each person holds his own place each one helps the other, who does not provide enough for himself, and vice versa, and this in a variety of ways physically, mentally, but also socially. "The peace of the city is an ordered peace of the citizens between those who command and those who obey," as Augustine says in the nineteenth book of the *City of God*.[333]

The owning of possessions derives from positive law, since following natural law "the possession of all is in common," as is said by Isidore in book seven of the *Etymologies*.[334] The same is said in Augustine's *On John*[335] and in distinction eight canon one, we see: "according to the law a human says this: 'this villa is mine, this slave is mine, this house is mine.' Human laws are the laws of the emperors."[336] Natural law is preferred over positive law just as the origin is preferred over the principle; because of this the final canon of distinction nine says: "constitutions, therefore, either ecclesiastical or secular, if they are proven to be contrary to natural law, must be completely abolished."[337] Therefore for the good of peace it is allowed to confiscate private property against the will of the owner.

---

[332] Aristotle *Nicomachean Ethics* IX.9 1169a (Panella). Cf. Remigius dei Girolami *De Bono Communi*

[333] Augustine *De Civitate Dei* XIX.13 8-9.

[334] Isidore *Etymologiae* V.4.

[335] Augustine *Super Iohannem* Tractatus III.21.

[336] *Decretum Gratiani* Distinctio VIII Canon I

[337] *Decretum Gratiani* Distinctio IX Canon XI.

The Counterargument: That which supplies the defect of another seems to excel that which is deficient. But the law of men supplies the means of determining natural law, and so it seems that natural law is deficient, for example positive law states that such and such a sin is to be punished with such and such a punishment; according to natural law, however, we have only generally that all sins are to be punished. Therefore, natural law is not to be preferred to positive law, but rather the opposite.

The Response: The origin, in as much as it is discussed simply, is always to be preferred to the principle in as much as it is the origin, certainly, however, following this, the opposite can be true, since whatever the principle has as the principle, it has it from the origin. He who knows the conclusion understands more than he who only knows the question, nevertheless knowledge of the question is nobler and more certain than the knowledge of the conclusion.

Certainly, too, while the number surpasses oneness in quantity, nevertheless unity surpasses the number simply in nobility. Human law is derived from natural law just like the conclusion from the question, for example: homicide is prohibited – this derives from natural law, which prohibits that anyone from killing another – or like a specific is derived from a general, for example since, as was discussed before, such and such a punishment is given for such and such a crime, derives from the general principle that all crimes are to be punished.

The fourth argument is made with respect to the Catholic Church, whose good consists in the peace of the faithful, just as the good of the body consists of the peace of the limbs and the good of a household consists of the peace of the members of the household.

The church is called the body of Christ, as is said in *Colossians*: "He Himself is the head of the body of the church;" and again "for His body, which is the church." [338]It is also called the house of God, as is said in first *Timothy*: "to abide in the house of the Lord, which is the church of the living God."[339] And according to eighth book of the *Etymologies* of Isidore, *ecclesia* in Greek means *convocatio* in Latin, that is an assembly, and *catholica* means *universalis*,[340] that is whole, since certainly the whole flock of the faithful is called together from the whole world into a peaceful unity of faith for the experiencing of the universal good, which is God; just as there is one faith, as is said in *Ephesians*: "one faith,"[341] so is there also one church, as is discussed in *Song of Songs*: "my dove is unique"[342] etc... *Glossa*: "great is the praise of universal unity."

Therefore the good of the church relies on the peaceful union of the faithful, just as the Collect says: "those to whom you gave faith You also gave peace;"[343] another states: "Your church, brought together by the Holy Spirit,

---

[338] *Collosians* 1:18.

[339] I *Timothy* 3:15.

[340] Isidore *Etymologiae* VIII.1.

[341] *Ephesians* 4:5.

[342] *Song of Songs* 6:8.

[343] From the Collect for the Monday following Pentecost: *Deus qui Apostolis tuis Sanctum dedisti Spiritum.*

is troubled in no way by attacks."[344] *Acts of the Apostles* also says: "the church was enjoying peace throughout Judea."[345] Judea can be interpreted to mean "confessing," since it can refer to the confession of faith. So the apostle says in first *Corinthians* and in second *Corinthians*: "to the church of God which is in Corinth etc... grace and peace be with you."[346] The ecclesiastical good is to be preferred over the temporal good, just as the head of the church, that is the pope, is to be preferred over the head of the temporal power, that is, over the emperor.[347]

The Counterargument: The church prohibits this very thing, as Innocent III decreed in the general council[348] in *Extravagantes* book three title thirteen: "to lay people and to clergy the power to take away goods from the church is in no way given."[349] The same is seen in *Extravagantes* book three title forty nine chapter four, which begins *Non minus*, and chapter 7, which begins *Adversus consules*. Etc...[350]

The Response: The church is exempted in the case of public use; so is said in that same chapter, which begins *Non minus*: "unless the bishop and the clergy should see such a great necessity or use that, without any coercion, in order to relieve common utility or necessity, where the resources of the laity are insufficient, they may give sub-

---

[344] From the Collect for the Friday in the Ember Week (the Quattor Tempora) of Pentecost: *Da, quaesumus, ecclesiae tuae misericors Deus..*

[345] *Acts of the Apostles* 9:31.

[346] I *Corinthians* 1:2-3 and II *Corinthians* 1:1-2.

[347] One of the few places Remigius dei Girolami lays out his support for the Pope over the emperor.

[348] The Lateran Council 1215.

[349] *Liber Extravagantes* Liber III Titulum XIII Capitulum XII.

[350] *Liber Extravagantes* Liber III Titulum LXIX Capitulum IV and XII.

sidy from the church's goods;"[351] *Glossa*: "they should give just as other owners for the construction of a road or for the building and maintenance of bridges." Ecclesiastical goods can, then, be received by the laity for the much greater good of peace.

The Counterargument: In the same chapter, which begins *Adversus consules*, is added: "because of the foolishness of certain people, the Roman pontiff must be consulted first, whose interest is in providing for the common use."[352]

The Response: This needs to be understood as being true unless the premier high priest, that is Christ, whose vicar is the pope, wishes the opposite, since "one should obey God more then men," as is said in *Acts of the Apostles*.[353] God, as well as divine law, prefers the good of peace to all temporal goods.

The Counterargument: But in the *Liber Sextus* book three, which begins *Gratuimus*, all clerics who give such things to lay people are excommunicated unless they have specially given permission from the apostolic chair.[354]

The Response: Pope Benedict XI modified this decree in his constitution, which begins *Quod olim*. He wishes that excommunication be imposed on only those people who were compelled to hand over the goods, not those who gave freely or who received goods freely given.[355]

---

[351] *Liber Extravagantes* Liber III Titulum LXIX Capitulum IV.

[352] *Liber Extravagantes* Liber III Titulum LXIX Capitulum VII.

[353] *Acts of the Apostles* 5:29.

[354] *Liber Sextus Decretalium* Liber III Titulum XXIII Capitulum III.

[355] Benedict XI *Quod Olim* Perugia 12th of May 1304 (Panella).

The Counterargument. But in this constitution it is added that the Lateran Council should be supplemented by consulting the supreme pontiff in such matters.

The Response. Without doubt the pope is to be obeyed and he is certainly to be consulted in the aforementioned circumstances. In every case, however where it is known for sure that something goes against love, neither the laws of men nor excommunication are to be feared, since in no way is something to be done against love, the effect of which is peace.

The Counterargument. But in the *Liber Sextus*, book three, which begins *Prohibemus*, the goods of the church are prohibited from being submitted to lay people.[356]

The Response. It must be said that in such a case it does not seem proper to call it the submission of the church, but rather the relief, since it is for the good of the community and for peace, to which no other good is equal, however the order of law and of love declares that the church is always consulted as a superior.

The fifth argument is made with respect to the final cause.

The purpose is that which is desired the most, according to the philosopher.[357] Peace also should be desired by all, according to Augustine in the nineteenth book of the *City of God* and chapter nine of Dionysius' *On the Divine Names*, and therefore, in a way, it is a purpose.[358] Because of this the *Psalm* says "He who gives your lands peace,"[359]

---

[356] *Liber Sextus Decretalium* Liber III Titulum IX Capitulum II.

[357] For example in the *Metaphysics* and the *Nicomachean Ethics*.

[358] Augustine *De Civitate Dei* XIX.13 and Ps. Dionysius the Areopagyte c.9.

[359] *Psalm* 147:14.

since, that is, the peace of the road is the purpose on the road, and the peace of the fatherland is its ultimate and perfect purpose; and therefore he says in the plural "lands." The purpose is preferred to those things which lead to the purpose. Therefore, all other goods must be set aside for the good of peace.

The Counterargument. The cause is preferred to the effect; but the purpose is an effect of the cause being complete; therefore, the completion of the cause is preferred over the purpose.

That which is moving in actuality is preferred over that which moves metaphorically, (since actuality is primary over metaphor, and so metaphorical movment is supplementary), because of this saying that 'the man laughs' is simply more excellent than saying 'the meadow laughs.' But according to the philosopher in the second book of the *On Generation and Corruption* that which is finishing does so with actual movement while the purpose moves metaphorically.[360] Therefore etc...

The purpose of medicine and the medical arts is the health of the body, nevertheless both of these are preferred over their purpose; the doctor is a being of reason while the health of the body is an accident and lacking in reason; in the same way the art of medicine is a perfection of the mind, but the health of the body is a perfection of the body. The substance, however, is simply to be preferred over the accident, the rational to that which lacks reason and the perfection of the soul to the perfection of the body. Therefore the purpose is not always to be preferred to those things which lead to the purpose.

---

[360] Actually Aristotle *De Generatione et Corruptione* I.7 (Panella).

The Response. There are four causes, which have a relative progression of importance in four steps and exist in twofold combination. These are: material, form, effect and purpose.

Among these, the purpose holds the first step, which is the cause of causes, according to the philosopher. The second step is the effective cause, which moves matter to the reception of form, being moved by consideration toward its purpose. The formal cause holds the third step, which, while begun by the effective cause, completes it in material form. The material cause holds the final step, which is potential existence, according to the philosopher, and is near nothing, according to Augustine in book twelve of the *Confessions.*[361]

The first combination is between the material and formal cause. The formal cause is the formal cause of matter, and, on the other hand, the material cause is the material cause of form; while the formal cause is nobler than the material since it sets it in motion and perfects it, but the converse is also true, albeit secondarily, since the material sustains form.

The second combination is between the effective cause and the purpose. While both of them cause themselves in a sense, the purpose causes the effect simply and originally, in as much as completion has no motion unless it is motion toward the purpose. But the effect causes the purpose secondarily, since its movement brings the purpose to pass, but nevertheless it is by virtue of the purpose that it primarily moves itself.

---

[361] Augustine *Confessions* XII.6 14-15.

It must also be said that actuality is nobler than metaphor, nevertheless it does not follow that actual movement is nobler than metaphorical movement. The entirety of nobility is not contained in movement, otherwise some other nobility would have increased for God when He began to move creatures in time. Greater nobility is found in existence, since it has a purpose in respect to the effective cause, which was shown above. Therefore the objection is not proven, since the metaphor is understood in accordance with a thing of inferior nobility and not accordance with a thing of superior nobility; just as the syllogism: "Adamant is a stone in actuality, Christ, however, is a stone metaphorically, therefore adamant is nobler than Christ" does not follow.

Thirdly, according to the philosopher in book two of *On the Soul*[362] and the commentary concerning this passage by Themistius, purpose is twofold, that is "which" and "for which."[363] That which is desired as the purpose is not unsuitable, since it would be less noble than that which is arranged toward the end, just as Themistius discusses concerning health and happiness which is inherent. Every perfection of the body and of the soul is certainly less noble than the body and the soul themselves, since the substance is nobler than the accident; which happens to occur, since that is not the ultimate purpose.

The ultimate purpose is subjected to that for which such a purpose is desired. Health, for example, just as Themistius said, is striven for in order to be healthy and happiness in order to be happy. Therefore health is not the purpose of medicine and the medical arts unless in as

---

[362] Aristotle *De Anima* II.4 415b 2-3 and 20-21.
[363] Themistius *In De Anima* III.

much as it is ordered toward the perfection of a human, since the soul is not perfected by the medical arts nor the body by health, unless in as much as the soul and the body are of a human, who is himself simply nobler than any accidental perfection of his own.

The sixth argument is made with respect to the ruler.

He who may lawfully require temporal goods for a small good and sentence a fine for a small ill may do so much more lawfully for a great good and a great ill. He who rules, be it a king or some other lord, may require temporal goods lawfully from his subjects for a smaller good than peace, for example for a journey, for a bridge, for a militia, for the marriage of a daughter, etc..

Therefore, he is much more able to do this for peace. In the same way he may condemn his subjects for smaller offenses than if they oppose peace, that is wage war, for example for theft and for assault, etc... Therefore, he may punish them all the more for waging war.

The Counterargument. Since it is not always true that he who can do less is also able to do more; it does not seem to follow that he who can require for small things can also require for great things.

The Response. The ability to require for small matters is not a small power, but a greater power and similarly the ability to require for greater matters is not a greater power, but a lesser power, just like the ability to enter through a smaller door is greater than the ability to enter through a large door, and just as the ability to see a small letter is greater than the ability to see and read a large one and just as the ability to overcome enemies with few arms and soldiers is a greater ability than being able to overcome them with many weapons and a great host.

A Second Counterargument. It is also not always true that he who can do more can also do less. So for example the intelligent man, who can understand universal principles, which are greater, nevertheless cannot understand a single direct principle, which is lesser, and which the sense, a power inferior to the intellect, understands.

A soldier can fight the whole day long and give great blows with the sword, this is greater than being able to carry a great load on his shoulder, be it of wool or some other material, which the soldier cannot do; nevertheless, a strong worker is able to do this, who is of a lesser status in society than the soldier is. A man inclined to science is able to study and meditate in solitude all day long, this is greater than being able to dig in the field, which he is not able to do; nevertheless, a farmer is able to do this, who is of a lesser station in society than the man inclined to science.

The Response. He who is able to do more is always able to do less when more and less are in reference to the power of the operator; for example he who is able to carry one hundred books is able to carry ten, and he who is able to understand subtleties is able to understand blatant things and he who is able to confer orders is able to absolve sins. The same holds true of power in a hierarchy, in which what the inferior can do the superior can do as well; for example: that which the proconsul can do the emperor can as well and that which a bishop can do the pope can as well.

Nothing prohibits anything from being superior in an absolute sense, because it is inferior in some way, just as the human body is in an absolute sense more noble than iron, and nevertheless iron, in a certain sense, is more noble than the human body because it is hard and the human body is soft. It can also be said that that which is inferior, since it is lesser, can also be superior, but in a more noble manner; for example a someone can be poor through the work of their own hands, but can be rich through commanding the hands of others; and someone can sense in a limited way, but can think in an open way, and vice versa since the intellectual part commands the sensitive part.

Conclusion

Finally it must be noted that in such amnesties as are discussed above, the intent for them to be extended to sustained loss is not seen when the spoil still remains in the hands of a pillager and this person is known as one, especially when he is an indigent.According to Seneca in the book *On Mercy* a prince should conduct himself in the manner of a doctor.[364] Therefore, just as a doctor conserves, as much as he can, the good of each individual member with the common good of the human body, so the prince should conserve the good of each citizen unharmed, as much as he can, with the good of the body of the people, so that he be at least provided from the treasury for such injury, if amnesties from injury be extended to all universally without exception.

Here ends the treatise on the good of peace by Brother Remigius of Florence, a teacher of theology of the Dominican order.

---

[364] Seneca *De Clementia* III.3.

Texts Cited in the *De Bono Pacis*

I. Classical References

Aristotle *De Anima* – 135; 145

Aristotle *De Generatione et Corruptione* – 143

Aristotle *Nicomachean Ethics* – 128; 132; 137; 143

Aristotle *Metaphysics* – 134; 135; 143

Aristotle *Politics* – 135; 136

Cicero *De Oficiis* – 129

Cicero *Oratio in Catilinam Priam in Senatu Habita* – 129

Ps. Cicero *Invecta contra Salustium* – 128

Ps. Dionysius the Areopagyte *De Divinis Nominibus* – 143

Seneca *De Clementia* – 149

II. Old Testament References

Psalms – 143

The Wisdom of Solomon – 132

Song of Songs – 139

Isaiah – 132

Jeremiah – 131

II *Maccabees* – 129

III. New Testament References

Matthew – 132; 133

Luke – 133

John – 129

The Acts of the Apostles – 133; 139; 141

I *Corinthians* – 129; 140

II *Corinthians* – 140

Ephesians – 131; 139

Collosians – 139

I *Timothy* – 139

IV. Patristic References

V. Miscellaneous References

The Nine Sermones de Pace

Introduction to the Nine Sermons on Peace[365]

Like the *De Bono Pacis*, the nine *Sermones de Pace* is concerned with discussing the good of peace. Each of these sermons begins with a passage of Scripture: 1. Psalm 122:7; 2. Job 25:2; 3. Mark 9:49; 4. and 6. Psalm 147:14; 5. Philippians 4:7; 7. Luke 11:21; 8. Mark 5:34 and 9. Psalm 67: 14-15. These passages are then examined as to how they promote peace as the highest good. In addition to the difference in the organization, there are, for example, no counterarguments and solution presented, as the sermons are to be heard rather than read and a complex structure is not needed, one notable difference between the texts is in the choice of authority. Like the *De Bono Communi*, the *De Bono Pacis* relies heavily on the works of Aristotle and other Classical sources, while the context of the sermons lends itself better to the use of Scriptural sources and the writings of church fathers such as Augustine.

Perhaps the most striking aspect of the sermons, however, is the personal and political information that comes through in several of the sermons. Where the *De Bono Pacis* and the *De Bono Communi* are nearly silent on the direct political problems of the city, contenting themselves with a more generalized discussion, and are completely silent regarding Remigius dei Girolami himself, three sermons discuss not only the importance of peace but Girolami's life and times. Sermon V is a touching farewell to his community before departing on a journey, in which he wishes them peace; Sermon VI gives a bit of an insight into how a sermon comes to be, as he chooses a

---

[365] The Latin text I used for this translation is from the edition in Panella (2014), 248-275. This edition also contains copious notes and a translation into Italian.

passage from vespers of that day; Sermon IX seeks to re-solve a dispute between the clergy of Florence and the Dominicans, here, like in the other political treatises, Re-migius does not discuss in detail what the issue is, but seeks to exhort both sides to cooperati

The Nine Sermons on Peace

by Brother Remigius dei Girolami O.P.

Sermon I

"Let there be peace in your virtue" As it says in the *Psalm*.[366]

Without the virtue of God, we cannot begin to understand the word of God, as it says in second *Corinthians*: "we are not sufficient ourselves to understand anything on our own, but this ability comes from God."[367] Likewise without the virtue of God we cannot show forth that which we have understood, as it says in the *Psalm*: "The Lord will give the word to those preaching the good news with great vir-

---

[366] *Psalm* 122:7.
[367] II *Corinthians* 3:5.

tue."[368] So too, without the virtue of God we would not have been able to do those things which seem virtuous, as is said in the *Psalm*: "He will give the voice of virtue to His voice,"[369] and therefore etc.

Let there be. This phrase is spoken by the prophet David to God and can be understood as discussing the entire procession to Christ, there are three things which come together in this procession: prayer on account of the *let there be*, concord on account of the *peace* and beginning on account of *in your virtue*; that is: prayer, accord and birth. The first is in voice and should also be in the heart, the second is in intention and the third is in reason.

Concerning the first, prayer is seen to be efficacious for four reasons, the first reason is from the holiness of the ones praying: "great power has the prayer of the just man," as is said in *James*,[370] but the prayer of sinners are not effective, but harmful, they do not profit but hinder, as Gregory says: "Since He it is who scatters"[371] etc., and in *John*: "God does not hear sinners"[372] since "he who does not incline their ear" etc. as is said in *Proverbs*.[373] The second reason for the efficacy of prayer is number, since two are more able than one, as is said in *Matthew* "if two of you" etc.;[374] Far more are three and ten and a hundred and a thousand etc.; for this reason the church prays: "granting on behalf of many intercessors." The third is unity, since many are not more powerful than a few unless the

---

[368] *Psalm* 67:12.

[369] *Psalm* 67:34.

[370] *James* 5:16.

[371] Gregory the Great *Regula Pastoralibus* III.7.

[372] *John* 9:31.

[373] *Proverbs* 29:9.

[374] *Matthew* 18:19.

many are in some way united. A thousand soldiers can defeat two thousand if the two thousand are divided in mind. If some soldier thrusts his spear to the front and another behind, or one to the right and another to the left, they are less powerful than one alone. For the same reason virtue is stronger united than it is when dispersed, as is said in the book *On Causes*,[375] which makes this clear by citing many examples. The fourth reason is in crying out, as is said in the *Psalm*: "I have cried to the Lord in my distress and he has heard me,"[376] and again: "I have cried out to the Lord with my voice, with my voice I have made intercession."[377] This voice is not required on account of God, since He sees the heart, nor is the crying out necessary on His account, since He has heard perfectly and is closer to us than we are ourselves, according to Augustine; but these are necessary on our account, so that devotion may grow greatly in our hearts, since, just as Augustine says in his *Letter to Probus*: "By words and other signs are our minds brought higher."[378] In this procession are good men, that is the members of religious orders and the priests etc., many in their kind, but one in their wish for peace and they bear great cries; and therefore it must be hoped that God will bring peace about.

Every human intends peace, according to Augustine and Dionysius, but certain ones want a true peace, others only an apparent and false peace, as is true for the good as well. Thence those who are delighted in wars, which they undertake on account of the false peace of honor, and the

---

[375] Ps. Aristotle *De Causis* 17.
[376] *Psalm* 119:1.
[377] *Psalm* 141:2.
[378] Augustine *Ad Probam* II.4.

same for other sinners; *Isaiah* says: "there is no peace for the wicked."[379] Peace is "ordered concord," as Augustine says in book nineteen of *The City of God.*[380]

It must be understood, concerning the third , that every created good originates from the highest uncreated good, so *James* says: "every [gift] is given"[381] etc. So peace, which is the highest good and seeks reconciliation between opponents, as Augustine and the Philosopher say, cannot exist unless through God's virtue through which every discord is healed and every enmity pacified, however great in power one party may be, or how greatly offended or how longstanding the enmity,[382] since it is pacified by God's virtue through the blood of Christ. Through this the all powerful God, whose least offense supersedes every offense of every creature, who, for more than five thousand years, was enemy of man, is reconciled with man, as is said in *Colossians*: "reconciling through the His blood on the cross whether in heaven or on earth."[383] Therefore, no one ought to despair that with God's virtue, by the merits of the prayers of the saints, every war may be brought to peace, and this imperfectly in life and nevertheless perfectly in the fatherland. To which be peace etc.

---

[379] *Isaiah* 48:22.
[380] Augustine *De Civitate Dei* XIX.13. Cf. Remigius dei Girolami *De Bono Pacis* II.
[381] *James* 1:17.
[382] Cf. Remigius dei Girolami *De Bono Pacis* II.
[383] *Colossians* 1:20.

Sermon II

Power and terror belongs to Him who makes concord in His high places, as is said in the book of *Job.*[384] [Panella identifies this as Sermon IV of the series *Ad Priores Civitatis*][385]

Sermon III

Have salt amongst yourselves and be at peace with one another, as is written in *Mark.*[386]

In order for the congregation to have true peace, the salt of discretion is especially necessary, so that the friar or the prelate knows to discern between place and place, time and time, person and person, manner and manner, cause and cause. This is so, since it is often the case that something ought to be done in one place and time and with one person and in one way and for one reason and not to be done in another place and time or with another person or in another way and for another reason. Truly to adopt equality of quantity in these things would be to adopt inequality of proportion, without which true peace is impossible, as is said in *Isaiah*: "peace will be the work of justice."[387]

In the same way, it is befitting that he knows to discern between nature and sin, between faults and persons, between humans and demons, between God and the creation, that is the world, between consciousness and fame. Indeed peace must be had with nature, not with sin, with persons not with faults, with humans not with demons, with God not with the world, with consciousness, not

---

[384] *Job* 25:2.
[385] Cf. Panella (2014), 132-133.
[386] *Mark* 9:49.
[387] *Isaiah* 32:17.

with fame that goes against the conscience, so is says in the *Psalm*: "I shall pursue my enemies and I shall overtake them, and I shall not turn aside until they fall; I shall destroy them so that they shall not be able to stand, they shall fall under my feet."[388]

For this reason a prelate ought most to fight against wickedness which is committed in the home or outside of the home, in the choir etc...; and if something is sought immorally, he must not listen even if it is sought by his greatest friend, for which reason Tullius writes in his *On Friendship*: "this law is established irrevocably so that we do not request wicked things nor do them when asked."[389] Or you could say that salt has a triple nature: it is irritating, that is it acts as the conscience does; it is a preservative, that is it acts as the study of sacred Scripture does; and it is a condiment, that is through a discreet life, and above all a discreet tongue.

Sermon IV

Who gives your borders peace and satiates you with the best of grain, as is said in the *Psalm*.[390]

He shows forth the highest good, that is, peace in the phrase: *Who gives your borders peace* and He shows forth its usefulness in the phrase: *satiates you with the best of grain*.

Concerning the first point, the purpose is the highest good for each person, according to the Philosopher, since not even those things which are approaching the purpose

---

[388] *Psalm* 17: 38-39.
[389] Cicero *De Amicitia* c.12. Cf. Remigius dei Girolami *De Bono Communi* XVI.
[390] *Psalm* 147:14.

have excellence as such, but derive it from the purpose. He says *fines*, borders, in the plural since the fulfillment of the temporal congregation, whether of the city or of the castle or farm or hospices is temporal peace. For this reason, the rector must not quibble concerning peace, as the doctor concerning health, just as is said in the third book of the *Ethics*,[391] since peace is to be obtained without any quibbling. Similarly, the fulfillment of the spiritual congregation, for example a religious community, is spiritual peace.

Concerning the second point there are four advantages which apply:

1. The first advantage is temporal, since it says *who satisfies you with the best grain*, in other words, he nourishes with delicious and abundant foods, since He who fills every animal with blessing is in the midst of the congregation in peace, as *Matthew*: "Where two or three are gathered in my name"[392] etc... His name too is "prince of peace," as is said in *Isaiah*.[393] When, however, there is no peace in the congregation it is not satisfied, but often suffers loss. A disturbed brother, after all, is insufficient to take care of the community, indeed, he is ever hampered by force; they take back the proffered hand from the person to whom they offered it, since they are built up insufficiently by speaking discordantly; and God even does this in the fatherland. Thence the *Psalm* says: "scatter the

---

[391] Aristotle *Nicomachean Ethics* III.5 1112b.
[392] *Matthew* 8:20.
[393] *Isaiah* 9:6.

peoples who desire wars;"[394] he does not say "who do," since some are driven to wage wars by the ill will of adversaries.

2. The second advantage is sacramental. The Body of Christ cannot be made without bread made of grain, since this is the specific substance of this Sacrament. It says: *he satisfies with the best of grain* since, just as the Teacher says in the fourth book of the *Sentences*: "The Body of Christ renews and satisfies the inner man before the rest of the graces."[395] When is there a benefit of the sacrament which follows the participation in the sacrament, certainly this means grace, or the increase of grace. When the peace of the conscience is lacking, the participant is not filled, but poisoned, as it says in *Job*: "their bread is turned into asp's venom in their stomachs."[396]

3. The third advantage is spiritual, that is the words of God, and therefore applies to *who sends forth etc...*[397] Where this touches the principle of such an advantage, since this was said before to be abundant and diffuse, is in the effect, since sinners are converted from impotent ignorance and wickedness, as is made clear from what that follows in the psalm. When, however, peace is lacking from the

---

[394] *Psalm* 67:31.
[395] Peter the Lombard *Liber Sententiarum* IV. dist. 8. cap. 7 (Panella corrects this from dist. 9 which is given in the text).
[396] *Job* 20:14.
[397] *Psalm* 147:15.

conscience, the heart grows hot, the foot slows, the tongue trembles to speak, but it is not believed by the hearer; because of this it is not satisfied, but emptied out and vexed.

4. The fourth is celestial, since "Blessed are the peacemakers..." as it says in *Matthew.* "...since they shall be called the children of God."[398] When, however, there is no peace this vision is not fulfilled, but comes to nothing, as is said in *Hebrews.* "Live at peace and in sanctity with everyone, without which no one will see God."[399] *Isaiah* 48:22 says as well: "There is no peace for the impious, says the Lord."[400] More is made of the impious through mercy. And therefore etc...

Sermon V

May the peace of God which surpasses all understanding keep your hearts and minds, as is said in *Phillipians.*[401]

I am leaving for a while, but, God willing, going to return to you quickly. Therefore, that which the apostle wishes for the Philippians in these words set forth I wish for all of you as well.

My first wish for you is certainly peace, since it says *Peace*, without which there can be no good in the congregation.

My second wish for you is the truth of peace, since it says *of God.* Human peace, when God, who is truth, is ab-

---

[398] *Matthew* 7:9.
[399] *Hebrews* 12:14.
[400] *Isaiah* 48:22.
[401] *Phillipians* 4:7.

sent, is by necessity a false peace, since "all human things are false" as it says in *Psalms*: "He has himself seen our form."[402] For this reason too it says in *Ezechiel*: "They say peace and there is no peace."[403]

My third wish for you is the substantiality of peace, since it says: *which surpasses all understanding*, at least human understanding. He who supports himself on human understanding cannot have true peace, since "God Himself is our peace," as is said in *Ephesians*.[404] Because of this it often happens to humans that when they strive with human understanding for a quiet and peaceful life, these people meet with wars and litigations against them on all sides.

My fourth wish for you is the use of peace, since it says: *may He guard your hearts*, that is as far as the desire for good, and *your minds*, that is as far as the understanding of truth; which two things are the most useful for humans since without these it is not possible to be whole, nor to have these two things without peace, through which men are ordered in spirit both in respect to themselves and in respect to their opponents.

In my absence my subprior will act as my vicar etc...

Sermon VI

Who gives your borders peace and satiates you with the best of grain, as is said in *Psalms*.[405]

This will be sung today at Vespers. Two things in the above passage pertains to the eucharist as well; of these

---

[402] *Psalm* 115:11 and *Psalm* 102:14.
[403] *Ezechiel* 13:10.
[404] *Ephesians* 2:14.
[405] *Psalm* 147:14.

two the first is the preface of peace that is undertaken before the eucharist, since it says: *Who gives your borders peace*; the second of these is the sacrament of the eucharist, which is to be assumed that this is indicating, since it says: *and satiates you with the best of grain*.

In the first case, the prophet refers to three things. First the author of peace, since he says: *who*, that is God and Lord, concerning whom was spoken before; thence *Isaiah* says: "I the Lord create peace,"[406] and in the *Psalms*: "Let there be peace in your virtue."[407] He refers to the order of peace, since he says: *places*, as placement includes order, as is discussed in the *Six Principles*. "Position is the certain position of the parts and the order of generations."[408] When things are not ordered by their nature according to urgency, they are not able to have peace, for example when heavy elements ascend upward, like earth and water –this causes storms in the air: winds, hail, thunder, lightning and suchlike – or when lighter elements descend, for example when the air pushes down into the earth –this creates storms in the earth, earthquakes for example. For this reason Augustine says in book nineteen of the *City of God* that: "peace is the harmonious order of humans."[409] Since sin lies in the taking away of quantity, of type and of order, as Augustine says..., no sinner can have true peace, as is said in *Isaiah*: "there is no peace for the impious, says the Lord,"[410] and

---

[406] *Isaiah* 45:7.

[407] *Psalm* 121:7.

[408] Attributed to Gilbertus Porretanus *Liber Sex Principiorum* VI.60.

[409] Augustine *De Civitate Dei* XIX.13. Cf. Remigius dei Girolami *De Bono Pacis* III.

[410] *Isaiah* 48:22.

"the beginning of every sin is pride," as it says in *Ecclesi-astes*,[411] this is the reason that Solomon says in *Proverbs* that there are "always quarrels"[412] among the proud. Since pride is most often apparent in the desires for rulership, thus it is that Augustine says in the *Glosa* to *Psalms* that the throne of pestilence is the love of rulership.[413] He touches on the noblest quality of peace, since he says *your borders*. A border is the best in each individual, according to the Philosopher. But he says *borders* in the plural since borders imply a certain order. Temporal peace, certainly itself would be a border, nevertheless what is beyond is ordered to borders as temporal peace is ordered to the peace of the heart, and the peace of the heart to the peace of eternity. Therefore the peace of the heart is a preface that precedes the eucharist, without which he who goes up to the sacrament "eats and drinks judgment for him-self,"[414] since: "His place is made in peace."[415]

Concerning the second point he refers to two things. The first is the material of this sacrament since he says: *grain*; there is, after all, no sacrament without bread made of grain. The second is the double efficacy of this sacra-ment. One of these comes from the restoration of the mind by the delight of the sacrament, since he says: *the best*; for this reason *Jeremiah* says: "I will fill the souls of the priests with plenty."[416] The priest must be he who cel-ebrates this sacrament. The second comes from the resto-ration of the mind by abundance, since he says: *satisfies*

[411] *Ecclesiastes* 10:15.
[412] *Proverbs* 13:10.
[413] Glosa to *Psalm* 1:1.
[414] I *Corinthians* 31:14.
[415] *Psalm* 75:3 of the Latin Vulgate.
[416] *Jeremiah* 31:14.

you; for "The Body of Christ renews and satisfies the inner man before the rest of the graces," as the master says in book four of the *Sentences*.[417] He who ascends to the receive without a conscience that is at peace, he eats but is not filled, rather, he is emptied, as it says in *Isaiah*: "they will eat on the left, but will not be satisfied;"[418] they are not made fat, but emaciated. In which form it is said in second *Kings* to Amnon, who is certainly understood as wicked: "Why are you so diminished by thinness?"[419]

That we may better have peace of conscience, you should forgive me and I should forgive you.

Sermon VII

Those things or *all those things, which he possesses, are at peace* as is said in *Luke*.[420]

It is true that these words are spoken concerning the devil and the false peace of sinners, as the *Psalm* says: "seeing the peace of the sinners,"[421] which is not truly peace, but more overpowering than even war is, as is said in *Jeremiah* and *Ezechiel*: "they say peace, and it is not peace,"[422] and in *The Wisdom of Solomon*: "living in a great ignorant war, they call such a great evils peace."[423] Nevertheless, it is possible to discern in them the truth concerning God and true peace, which the Son of God came into the world to establish; for this reason at His birth the angels sang: "Glory etc..., peace to men of good

---

[417] Peter the Lombard *Liber Sex Sententiarum* Book IV dist. 8 cap. 7.
[418] *Isaiah* 9:20.
[419] II *Kings* 13:4.
[420] *Luke* 11:21.
[421] *Psalm* 72:3.
[422] *Jeremiah* 8:11 and *Ezechiel* 13:10.
[423] *The Wisdom of Solomon* 14:22.

will."[424] He comes into this word again both in the preparation of the eucharist and in the monastic congregation.

No one can receive the eucharist unless, existing in true peace, he is possessed by the Savior; since "In peace is His place made," as it says in *Psalms*.[425] True peace cannot exist in mortal sin, as it says in *Isaiah*: "there is no peace for the impious, says the Lord,"[426] but it exists solely in the just man, as it says in *The Wisdom of Solomon*: "peace is for those chosen by God."[427] Therefore he who ascends to the eucharist with a conscience weighed down by mortal sin ascends to it in judgment and to his own damnation, as it says in first *Corinthians*: "who eats and drinks unworthily, eats and drinks judgement unto himself."[428] Therefore it is necessary to purify oneself beforehand, so that, existing in true peace, one may receive the eucharist worthily, as it says in the *Psalms*: "Who places peace upon your borders and satiates you with the best of grain;"[429] i.e. in the *Glosa* the bread which descended from heaven.

He also comes into this word in the monastic congregation, for which the highest good is peace, since without it the congregation cannot exist well. For this reason the Savior often said to the congregation of apostles: "Peace be with you,"[430] as he instructed them to have peace in *Matthew* and in *Luke*: "peace be with this house."[431]

---

[424] *Luke* 1:2,14.
[425] *Psalm* 75:3.
[426] *Isaiah* 48:22.
[427] *The Wisdom of Solomon* 3:9.
[428] I *Corinthians* 11:29.
[429] *Psalm* 147:14.
[430] *Matthew* 10:2.
[431] *Luke* 10:5.

Many things create peace in a congregation. The first of these is the establishment of mutual enjoyment, in the same way as the artisan builds a house and as fire creates heat, as it says in the *Psalm*: "there is much peace for those who love."[432] The second is the conservation of patience in adversity – just as diet creates health, as it says in *Isaiah*: "behold in peace my bitterness was the most bitter;"[433] the one who is impatient in word and deed cannot have peace. The third is humility – as the earth creates a firm edifice, concerning which Augustine says: "when planning to build something of great height, think concerning the foundation of humility;"[434] for this reason the *Psalm* says: "let there be peace in your virtue"[435] that is in humility, which is the particular virtue of Christ, as it says in *Matthew*: "learn from me since I am gentle and humble of heart, and you will find rest for your souls."[436] The proud and ambitious man cannot have peace, as it says in *Proverbs*: "there is constant strife among the proud;"[437] and Bernard says: "O ambition, cross of the supplicants, how you twist all and please all!"[438] The fourth is leadership, which means displaying discretion and prudence – as a general of an army creates victory, and this is most important in the prelate. For this reason *Mark* says: "have salt among yourselves and be at peace with one another,"[439] and *Luke*: "to illumine etc... to lead

---

[432] *Psalm* 118:165.
[433] *Isaiah* 38:17.
[434] Augustine *Sermons on the Old Testament* VI
[435] *Psalm* 121:7.
[436] *Matthew* 11:29.
[437] *Proverbs* 13:10.
[438] Bernard of Clairveaux *Flores* PL 183 1202D.
[439] *Mark* 9:49.

our feet on the path of peace."[440] He who cannot discern between one person and another, between one place and another, between one time and another, between one quantity and another, between one cause and another, is unable to have peace. The fifth is justice, by prohibiting the removal of peace, just as a demolition worker makes a stone column to be torn down, as is said in *Isaiah*: "The work of justice was peace,"[441] injustice does not permit peace to be kept. The sixth is by removing the source of strife that is study and solitude – just as blindness and flight create containment or as the removal of wood extinguishes a fire, as is said in the *Psalm*: "who will give me wings"[442] etc... For him who is in the multitulde, rather than in solitude, it is normal to be disturbed, as it says in *Job*: "In the world you will have troubles, in me, however, peace,"[443] and in *Luke*: "Martha etc...,and you are troubled"[444] etc...

Sermon VIII

That which Jesus said to the woman suffering from a flow of blood for twelve years is written in *Mark*: *Go in peace and be healed from your ills.*[445] Here it is intimated that, just as she receives physical health, so she receives peace for the metaphorical body of the state, of society or of the congregation.

And we say, that each individual leader creates peace first of all, at a most basic level by acting like a learned

---

[440] *Luke* 1:79.
[441] *Isaiah* 32:17.
[442] *Psalm* 54:7.
[443] *Job* 17:16,33.
[444] *Luke* 10:41.
[445] *Mark* 5:34.

doctor, as is said in *Isaiah*: "the prince of peace."[446] Secondly by the obedience of his subordinates, in the way that patients are obedient, without which the wisdom of the king or of the doctor cannot prevail; for this reason *Isaiah* says: "if only you had heeded my commandments! Your peace would have been like a river,"[447] and again: "if you turn from doing your own will you call the Sabbath delightful"[448] that is delicious rest; *Job* says "who has withstood him and has peace?"[449] *Proverbs* too says: "the obedient man is called victorious,"[450] and victory is followed by peace, as Augustine says in book nineteen of the *City of God*: "victory is the subjugation of the opposition, when this is done, there will be peace."[451] An example is given by Augustine in book five of the *City of God* of a king who beheads his own son, even though he was victorious, because he attacked contrary to his orders.[452]

The third thing that creates peace is love, as fire has natural love for conflagrations and heat, as is said in the *Psalm*: "there is great peace for those who love Your law;"[453] in this context, the first law is that God is to be loved above all others, from this law comes the common good, and from there comes a closer relationship with one's neighbor, since "there is no peace for the impious," as is said in *Isaiah*.[454]

---

[446] *Isaiah* 9:6.
[447] *Isaiah* 48:18.
[448] *Isaiah* 58:13.
[449] *Job* 9:4.
[450] *Proverbs* 21:18.
[451] Augustine *De Civitate Dei* XIX.12.
[452] Augustine *De Civitate Dei* V.18. This is the Roman general Torquatus, cf. Remigius dei Girolami *De Bono Communi* V.
[453] *Psalm* 118:165.
[454] *Isaiah* 57:21.

The fourth is the proof of this love through works, in the way that urine and the pulse and so forth are a proof of health, so that God may be honored in the creation of lofty churches, in the benefits of the clergy etc..., and the that the community may be honored in rewards, in excellent officials, etc..., and come to the aid of the religious poor and other beggars with public statutes. It is for this reason that Solomon, who is known as a peaceful king, honorably constructed a temple to God, as is described in third *Kings;* and in *Exodus* it says: "they offered peace offerings."[455] Another example of this is St. Ludovicus, the king of the Franks,[456] who cultivated peace within his kingdom through the charities he created. "Proof – that is a quantifiable sign – of love is in doing works," just as Gregory said.[457]

The fifth is in the use of fortifications, arms, laws and suchlike against enemies and criminals, in the same way that the fortifications of the body, clothing, houses and so on, shield the body from intemperate weather. For this reason, *Luke* states: "When the strong man guards the entrance to his home armed, all that he possesses remains at peace."[458]

The sixth is undertaking labors which are imposed for the common good, in suffering insults, and periodic injustices with patience, as in exercise there are incisions and bitter purifications, and as some dishes, of meat and of fish, are prepared with blows to become healthy for men;

---

[455] III *Kings* 6 and *Exodus* 32:6.

[456] Cf. Remigius dei Girolami *De Bono Communi* VIII.

[457] Gregory the Great *Sermo de Domenica Quarta in Quadragissima* 2:IX. 234a.

[458] *Luke* 11:21.

for this reason *Isaiah* 38:17 says: "behold in peace my bitterness is most bitter."[459]

The seventh is in abstaining from gaming with dice and from drinking in taverns and suchlike, since through these vices men are often driven to confusion one after the other, since "a tumultuous thing is drunkenness," as is said in *Proverbs*,[460] and again: "who has woe? Etc... Are they not the ones who delay in their cups?"[461] For this reason, as regards diet, the *Song of Songs* says: "there was a vineyard for the peacable,"[462] it does not say tavern, but "vineyard" since the vineyard is for the collecting of wine, while the tavern is for buying it.

The eighth is humility of spirit against the cancer of ambition, this acts like a bandage, or as a purgative, through which one is brought to passing stool.

The ninth is justice, which provides for the punishment of malefactors with fines, as an equivalent to a phlebotomy; in exiling the criminal, as an equivalent to purging the humors; or in execution, as an equivalent to the amputation of a limb; and in advancing the good, like a varied diet based on a variety of combinations. An example of this exists in Valerius.[463]

These nine things, then, create health: a wise doctor; an obedient patient, temperature returning to its natural state, showing proof, defensive barriers, effective medicine, a light diet, regulating purgatives, correct propor-

---

[459] *Isaiah* 38:17.
[460] *Proverbs* 20:1.
[461] *Proverbs* 23: 29-30.
[462] *Song of Songs* 8:11.
[463] Valerius Maximus *Factorum ac Dictorum Memorabilium*.

tions: *meinca simua diclipro*.[464] So health is understood from the point of view of the doctor, of the patient, from innate temperature, from proof, from defenses, from medications and this fourfold: 1. through the rising of bitter things, 2. through the taking away or washing off of sweet or savory things, 3. through the ejection of foul things, 4. through the observation of various circumstances, that is time, place, person, etc...

Sermon IX.

If you rest in the midst of the clergy, the wings of the dove shall be covered in silver and her back wings in the color of gold. While He who is in heaven appoints kings over her, snow shall fall in Selmon, as is said in the Psalm.[465]

We have come together in this way, dearest fathers and brothers, in order to rebuild peace between us, the Dominicans, and you the clergy of Florence, therefore I propose the words of the prophet David, which seem sufficient for this subject. First of all it bears on the clergy since it says: *If you rest in the midst of the clergy*, secondly it bears on the Dominicans, since it says: *the wings of the dove shall be covered in silver*, thirdly it bears on the maintenance of both since it says: *and her back in the color of gold* Fourthly it bears on the position of both parties, since it says: *while He who is in heaven appoints kings over her*, fifthly it bears on the famous reconcilia-

---

464 An acrostic made up of: "*m*edicus sapiens, *in*firmus obediens, *ca*lor ad naturam rediens, *si*gnum ostendens, *mu*nimen defendens, medicina *a*ffligens, *di*eta subtrahens, *cli*stere emictens, *pro*portio conrespondens" Panella.

465 *Psalm* 67:14-15.

tion between both parties, since it says: *snow shall fall in Selmon.*

Concerning the first and second it is worth noting that following the *Glosa* the dove is the church, since it says in *Song of Songs:* "one is my dove."[466] That it is one is an article of faith, as laid out in the *Creed:* "and in one holy catholic and apostolic Church."[467] In this dove there are some who are feet, meaning active members, as is said in *Psalms:* "our feet stand in your courts Jerusalem,"[468] and these courts certainly refer to the church. Others are feathers, that is contemplative members, as is said in *Psalms:* "who gives me feathers like the dove and I will both fly and rest?"[469] and again: "who walks on the wings of the winds."[470] Others are truly wings covered in silver, *Glosa:* "that is erudite with divine eloquence," this referes to preachers for whom, as Gregory said: "it is fitting that they absorb in contemplation, what they put forth in preaching;"[471] for this reason it says in *Psalms:* "the utterances of the Lord are true, like silver tested by fire."[472] This is especially true for the brothers of the Dominican order, who are preachers not only in fact, but are even devoted to it through their name. They are, therefore, both wings and feet. This is why in *Ezechiel* it says concerning preachers: "each one had four wings and their feet were straight, and the soles of their feet were like the

---

[466] *Song of Songs* 6:8.
[467] cf. the Nicene-Constantinopolitan Creed.
[468] *Psalm* 121:2.
[469] *Psalm* 54:7.
[470] *Psalm* 103:3.
[471] Cf. Gregory the Great *Regula Pastoralis.*
[472] *Psalm* 11:7.

soles of the feet of a calf;"[473] Gregory, speaking about this says: "not easily is the sermon of a preacher received if he seems to be less than moral."[474]

Therefore this passage should be directed to them in the vocative case: "O wings of the dove covered in silver" that is "O Dominican friars *if* etc...;" where it is to be noted that the conditional conjunction "if" sometimes denotes a necessity of thought, so in *Job*: "if you remain in my teachings, you will be my true disciples,"[475] here he seems to be saying: "since you ought to remain;" and in *Psalms*: "if you hear His voice,"[476] certainly this means that you should hear. This should be understood in the same way: "O Dominican friars, if you rest in the midst of the clergy" that is with the clergy and among them, or who ought to be the middle, that is the virtuous, since certainly you ought to rest. Rest, I said, that is to receive hospitality from them like a traveler, for whom it is right to live from the purse of the faithful, both laity and clergy, that is, to eat and drink with them and to lie in their beds. After food and drink follows sleep, as is said in the *Song of Songs*: "I ate etc... I drank"[477] etc... and following after: "I slept;" thence *Amos*: "you all sleep" that is, you ought to sleep "on beds of ivory"[478] that is in chaste beds, the beds of clergy, who ought to be chaste not only because of the obligation from this divine precept, but also from the personal vows made when being ordained to holy orders in the Western Church. Likewise, you ought to

---

[473] *Ezechiel* 1: 6-7.
[474] Cf. Gregory the Great *Regula Pastoralis*.
[475] *Job* 8:31.
[476] *Psalm* 94:8.
[477] *Song of Songs* 5:1-2.
[478] *Amos* 6:4.

rest with the clergy, that is, to sleep just as the quiet and peaceable, as is said in *Psalms*: "I will sleep and rest in that same peace."[479]

The clergy and the Dominicans walk about unarmed, since they are not warlike, but peaceable men, unless they are fighting against vice with those spiritual weapons of virtue, oration and the divine words. Then you ought to rest with the clergy, that is, be secure in speaking with them as if to a friend, as is said in *Job*: "you rest safely,"[480] and in *Ezechiel*: "you rest safely in the forests."[481] Especially between the clergy and the Dominicans there should exist friendship and love, both here and anywhere else, as in a community. For this reason, the canons of the great church in Besançon built our convent, and our prior had a voice in the election of the archbishop as a canon, until that time when one of the priors renounced this right due to his conscience.

For this reason, when the third subject is expressed: *and her back wings in the color of gold, Glosa*, that is in love: "through which every sorrow of the law shall be made light;" is said *her back wings* that is those back wings which are at the furthest part of the back of the dove. After all, according to book eleven of Isidore's *Etymologies*, it is from its durability that the back gets its name,[482] since it is the strongest for carrying and for enduring. "Love is patient and suffers all things," as is said in first *Corinthians*.[483] Just as gold excels every other

---

[479] *Psalm* 4:9.
[480] *Job* 11:18.
[481] *Ezechiel* 34:25.
[482] Isidore *Ethymologiae* XI.1.
[483] I *Corinthians* 13:4, 7.

metal, love itself excels the other virtues, which contains pallor, that is fear, putting the effect before the cause. When someone has more love, they have more filial fear as well, which considers the offense not the punishment, like the fear of a servant; for this reason the poet says: "love is a thing full of fear."[484]

This is certainly so since the love for God creates a literal pallor through the penitence of the body and through affliction it also creates a pallor and weakness from the absence of the beloved, compare Ovid's: "every lover is pale,"[485] and: "I am weak because of love" from the *Song of Songs*.[486] Every ill which arises for the lover is caused by the absence of the beloved, since the beloved is the greatest good for the lover. Love, therefore, in the absence of the beloved, wounds the lover, as it says in *Song of Songs*: "you have wounded my heart, my sister my love"[487] etc... It causes the lover to become weak, while the absence lasts, as it says in *Song of Songs*: "I am weak because of love."[488] This occurs because the lover has an emptiness in the eye of the mind, that is humility in thought and action, and in the eyes of the body through weeping and waking – as the dove also mourns through song --, and because the lover burns metaphorically in his interior flesh, that is the fervor of the mind, and in his bodily flesh because of continuous exercise and labor, and because the lover has no taste for food on account of the severity of his fasting; and again since "all flesh acts fool-

---

[484] Ovid *Heroides* I.12.
[485] Ovid *Ars Amatoria* I. 729.
[486] *Song of Songs* 2:5 and 5:8.
[487] *Song of Songs* 4:9.
[488] *Song of Songs* 2:5 and 5:8.

ishly because of the taste of the spirit," as Gregory said,[489] and he grows pale from this. Thirdly it causes the lover to die, as is said in *Song of Songs*: "love is strong as death,"[490] certainly the way the lover completely separates his heart from every other thing other than the beloved and dedicates his whole life to the beloved on account of their absence can be called death.

For this reason, love kills everyone since love is nothing other than the separation of those things which are joined together, as can be understood from the *Ecclesiastical Hierarcy*.[491] Nevertheless other books, as the *Glosa* says, have "in green" instead of "in the color." This pallor of the body comes from the greenness of the mind, that is, from the root of love, since, as Gregory says: "the branch of good works has no greenness, unless it is rooted in love."[492]

The kings, that is, the clergy and Dominicans are set above the dove, that is above the church, because of their understanding of heavenly things, that is Christ according to the *Glosa*, certainly so that the whole is put before the part, according to the rule of Ticonius, which Augustine discusses in his work *On Christian Doctrine*.[493] The clergy and the priests are kings and are crowned in the manner of kings, this corresponds to what is said in I *Peter*: "you are a chosen people, a royal priesthood;"[494] the very highest priest of his type is the lord bishop in his di-

---

[489] A quote attributed to Gregory the Great in Bernard of Clairveaux *Flores* PL 183 1200B.

[490] *Song of Songs* 8:6.

[491] Ps. Dionysius the Areopagyte *Ecclesiastice Ierarchie* c.7.

[492] Gregory the Great *Homilia in Evangelia* 27 (in CCSL 141: 229-230).

[493] Augustine *De Doctrina Christiana* III.30-37.

[494] I *Peter* 2:9.

ocese, since that which is sung in honor of blessed Germanus, whose feast day is celebrated today,[495] applies well to him, it is written in *Ecclesiastes*: "behold the great priest who in his days pleased God and was found to be just and in a time of wrath made reconciliation,"[496] through his eagerness and efforts and through his help and prayers, the peace following reconciliation may be better and sweeter than it was before the dissension and tumult.

In the same way a bowl of clay is more beautiful and better than it was before, when, after it breaks, it is repaired with filaments of silver; for this reason, the French vigorously destroy it, lest it become too great. The words of the lord bishop are filaments of silver, as is said in *Proverbs*: "the tongue of the just is choice silver."[497] Becoming great is the raising up of the mind, which is reduced from such a division. The cloth of the tunic of the Dominican is stronger when stitched where there was a rip in the cloth than the rest of the cloth which was not cut. So, the reconciliation after a division is a greater and more durable peace. Therefore, bishops are good rulers, and above kings, as blessed Ambrosius said to Theodosius the emperor, according to legend: "In the church I am the lord and you are as one of the common people." Rulers and above kings are the Dominicans as well, for while they preach to the rulers, they and the people are counted as one since they are ruled by the preaching of the Dominicans; for this reason, the *Glosa* says: "kings, that is, teachers."

---

[495] The 31st of July.
[496] *Ecclesiastes* 44.
[497] *Proverbs* 10:20.

This discord between the clergy and the Dominicans, who ought to be creating peace between the laity, is creating a great scandal among the people, who are themselves in discord. Infamy is called the blackening of fame, so Arrigetti says: "Which infamy blackened with horrible blemishes and water required great effort to wipe clean."[498] Restoration of good repute is also called wiping clean, which is also a fit name for reconciliation and peace, and therefore he says to whatever kings: *snow shall fall in Selmon*, which can certainly be understood as peace. Nothing is whiter than snow; indeed, elsewhere it says in *Psalms*: "you will wash me"[499] that is you, lord bishop, with the water of wisdom, "and I will be whiter than snow," since certainly the reputation of a good reconciliation will be better than it was before the division. Which for us etc...

---

[498] Arrigo da Settimello *De Diversitate Fortunae et Philosophiae Consolatione* I. 19-20.
[499] *Psalm* 50:9.

References in the *Sermones de Pace*

I. Classical References

Aristotle *Nicomachean Ethics* – 163

Ps. Aristotle *De Causis* – 158

Cicero *De Amicitia* – 162

Ovid *Ars Amatoria* – 181

Ovid *Heroides* – 181

Ps. Dionysius the Areopagyte *Ecclesiastice Ierarchie* – 182

Valerius Maximus *Factorum ac Dictorum Memorabilium* – 176

II. Old Testament References

Exodus – 175

Job – 160; 164; 173; 174; 179; 180

Ecclesiastes – 169; 182

II *Kings* – 170

III *Kings* – 175

Psalms – 157; 158; 163; 164; 166; 168; 169; 171; 172; 175; 180; 183

The Song of Songs – 176; 178; 179; 181

The Wisdom of Solomon – 181

Proverbs – 158; 169; 172; 174; 176; 182

Ezechiel – 166; 171; 180

Jeremiah – 169; 171

Isaiah – 159; 161; 165; 168; 169; 170; 171; 172; 173; 174; 175; 176

Amos -- 180

III. New Testament References

Matthew – 158; 163; 164; 170

Mark – 161; 173; 174

Luke – 171; 172; 173

John – 158

Hebrews – 165

Ephesians – 166

Phillipians – 166

The De Iustitia

Introduction to the *De Iustitia*[500]

1. Structure and Style of the Text

The text of the *Tractatus de Iustitia* appears on folios 206r-207r of the same manuscript that contains the *De Bono Communi* and the *De Bono Pacis*.[501] The *Tractatus de Iustitia* was written by Remigius dei Girolami as a couplet with his *Tractatus de Misericordia*. "When we had written the treatise on mercy, it seemed reasonable that this offered the opportunity to speak also to some extent concerning justice, that we may discuss how much the sun of justice has granted."[502] This creates an expectation in the reader that the primary function of this work is theological exegesis, rather than political theory. This expectation is reinforced in the final, sol iustitie concesserit, as the term sol iustitie is an epithet used for Christ. The focus of this text, then, would be the justice of God and how that manifests in what he has done in the history of Salvation. This is indeed not to say that there is no overlap between the theology of Remigius and his political ideology and that one of his works cannot be both a political and theological work. The two are inextricably linked and, in fact, all of Girolami's political works are also works of theology, relying heavily on the moral imperatives of a Christian to understand how a citizen should behave. However, what set the political works apart from the theological is the outcome, which informs the way a

---

[500] The Latin text I used for this translation is from the Capitani (1960) edition.

[501] Conv. Sopp. C.4.940 a the Biblioteca Nazionale. Davis (1960), pp. 664-665.

[502] de misericordia tractatum fecerimus, rationabile satis videtur ut offerente se opportunitate loquendi etiam de iustitia aliquid quantum sol iustitie concesserit disseramus

citizen or leader of a commune should understand themselves in relation to the commune, and how this affects the way in which they comport themselves.

The opening of the work creates uncertainty in the reader, concerning whether this text should be read as a theological or a political text. Like the *Sermons on Peace*, the *De Iustitia* opens with a scriptural quotation: "Love justice, you who judge the earth."[503] While a scriptural quotation would by no means be out of place in a work on theology, the reader who is aware of the other works of Remigius would realize that this does not preclude from being a political text. As the *De Bono Communi* also begins with a quotation from scripture, linking the two works together.

Interesting as well is the fact that there are, at least initially, few references to the works of Aristotle or other ancient philosophers and statesmen, such as Cicero, which are such a vital part of both the *De Bono Communi* and the *De Bono Pacis*. The first three texts Remigius discusses are Scriptural quotations, from *The Wisdom of Solomon*, *Psalms,* and *Proverbs* respectively. These quotations for a self-contained section in the text, which serve primarily to underscore the importance of justice for the Christian: "This is the chariot with which the Lord comes to us...and since it requires these that we may ascend through them to Him."[504] It is only through justice and mercy that a person can have an interaction with God.

Remigius dei Girolami makes the importance of justice and mercy even more poignant for his readers: "Disci-

---

[503] Diligite iustitiam qui iudicatis terram.
[504] Hec est enim bi qua dominus ad nos venit...et quod per ipsam ad eum ad eum accedamus requirit.

pline, that is justice and mercy, is mostly abandoned, even if it is kept by a few here and there."[505] That which is needed for a proper relationship with God, is then, mostly lacking. This again leads the reader back to the opening of the *De Bono Communi*: "...and there will be those who love themselves, who are greedy, puffed up and proud...this is seen clearly fulfilled in these times and in modern men and, alas, most of all in us Italians..."[506] Similar to the modern men in the *De Bono Communi*, humans have largely abandoned peace and justice in the *De Iustitia*.

A logical problem asserts itself. How can one be both just and merciful? The two, which are so closely associated by Remigius, seem to be at odds. The next section is spent discussing how it is possible for mercy and justice to coexist, and how being merciful informs the practice of being just. Especially important in this discussion is the idea of moderation, which Remigius demonstrates with a theological example: "Oneness is the midpoint between many extremes and truth the midpoint between many falsehoods. So, for example, the true faith holds the midpoint between Arius...and Sabellius."[507] For the remainder of the *De Iustitia*, the idea of moderation dominates. This idea is tied into a double understanding of the precepts of justice as both a negative and a positive command. Nega-

---

[505] Disciplina enim, idest iustitia et misericordia, multum destituitur si altera sine altera teneatur...

[506] ...erunt homines se ipsos amantes, cupidi, elati, superbi...hiis temporibus aperte videtur impleta in modernis hominibus et heu maxime in ytalicis nostris...

[507] Unum autem est medium inter plura extrema et veritas est medium inter plura falsa, ut inter Arrium...et Sabellium...veritas fidei tenet medium.

tive in the sense that one is never to commit an act of injustice, positive in the sense that one is supposed to carry out justice. It is the positive command that needs the temper, and Remigius compares the carrying out of justice, i.e. the punishment of crime, to the dispensing of medicine by a doctor, who: "...considers the time, for example if there is a waning quarter moon or if the dog star is in purification and so forth; he considers the place, for example, if the location is swollen or healthy..."[508] Like the physician has to moderate his practice depending on the circumstances, justice must be moderated depending on the circumstances, a crime may have to be overlooked or punishment might be delayed depending on the result of this justice, whether it results: "in good or in evil for the community..."[509]

The final section of the *De Iustitia* is a discussion of the various types that make up the positive commands of justice. This is an excellent example of both Remigius dei Girolami's dependence on Thomistic thought, and how he continues to develop these thoughts. In Thomas Aquinas: "there corresponded...a hierarchy of laws, divine, natural, and positive, with the last subdivided into canon and civil. Natural law and canon law proceeds from divine law, and civil law from natural law; unjust enactments were not law but iniquity."[510] Like Thomas Aquinas, he posits a twofold division in law, i.e. in justice, that is natural and positive. Whereas, divine law is under positive law: "Posi-

---

[508] considerat tempus, puta si est quarta luna in minutionibus et cetera; et si est canis in purgationibus et cetera; et considerat locum, puto si est locus egrotativus vel sanus et cetera...

[509] in bonum vel in malum communis...

[510] Davis (1960), pg. 671.

tive law too is double, that is divine and human and thus is double justice."[511] Both divine and human law are also subdivided, as is civil law that comes from human law: "Divine law too is double, that is old and new, as is human law, that is civil and ecclesiastical. Civil law too is double, that is imperial and municipal."[512] The only law that remains undivided is ecclesiastical law, which allows him to show, subtly here, but more explicitly in other works,[513] his support for the papacy in the Investiture conflict.

2. Relationship with the other Political Texts

If the opening of the *De Iustitia* creates an intertextual link with the opening of the *De Bono Communi*, it also reflects the difference in audience. The *De Bono Communi* is concerned with a more generalized audience, this is reflected in the very general opening.[514] This text is meant to bring all of the disparate parts of the community together, and in a sense, addressed to them. The carrying out of justice is confined to a much smaller portion of the population, and the *De Iustitia* begins with an exhortation to them.[515] Nevertheless, despite the specificity of this opening, the goal of both of these texts, as well as, the other political works is the same: "Virtue is to be loved on its own account; nevertheless it is not to end there, but to continue into the ultimate end, that is happiness and the

---

[511] positiva autem est duplex, scilicet divina et humana et sic est duplex iustitia.

[512] Divina autem est duplex, scilicet vetus et nova. Humana autem est duplex, scilicet civilis et ecclesiastica. Civilis autem est duplex, scilicet imperialis et municipalis.

[513] For example, in the *Contra Falsos Ecclesie Professores*.

[514] "in modern men, and alas most of all in us Italians."

[515] "Love justice, you who judge the earth."

highest good..."[516] This is not just a philosophical exposition on what the nature of justice is, but a guide as to how justice can be used to attain the summum bonum. What precicely is the summum bonum, however, is never discussed in the *De Iustitia*, rather one must look in the *De Bono Communi* and the *De Bono Pacis*. In chapter 9, among a number of other places in this text, of the *De Bono Communi*, Remigius discusses why the good of the many is to be loved more than the good of the one:

Of the first, the philosopher says in I *Ethics* that philosophers: "reported well the good which all desired;" and he says the same in many other places. Dionysius too says as much in the fourth chapter of *On the Divine Names*. From this certainly follows that the good of the community is to be loved more than the good of any individual, since the good of the community meets more with the highest good in common than the individual good.[517]

This *summum bonum* must then be understood in terms of Remigius dei Girolami's understanding of the part and the whole, an understanding that colors all of his political arguments. Since the part depends on the whole for its very existence, the whole is the more important, and therefore the good of the whole, the *bonum in commune* is more to be sought. It is the higher good than the

---

[516] virtus enim propter se amanda est, non tamen ibi sistendo, set in ulteriorem finem idest in beatitudinem et summum bonum ipsam referendo. Thomas Aquinas also discusses virtue as a means toward the *bonum communi*, c.f. *Summa Theologica* II.58.5-6.

[517] De primo dicit Philosophus in I Ethicorum quod philosophi «bene annuntiaverunt bonum quod omnia appetunt»; et idem dicit in pluribus aliis locis, et Dyonisius 4 c. De divinis nominibus. Ex quo certe sequitur quod bonum comune preamandum est bono particulari cuiuscumque tum quia bonum comune magis convenit cum bono sumpto in comuni quam bonum particulare

private good of the individual. In the *De Bono Pacis* as well, he discusses the good in more theological terms: "The good of God is preferred over the good of any one of His creatures. Peace is, however, the good of God." Peace then, is to be preferred over any temporal good. This same idea is seen in the fourth of his sermons on peace: "the goal is the highest good for each person, according to the philosopher...the fulfillment of the temporal congregation, whether of the city or of the castle or farm or monasteries is temporal peace...the fulfillment of the spiritual congregation, for example a religious community, is spiritual peace." The *summum bonum*, which every virtue is to lead to, is peace, to which the virtues of justice and mercy must lead. Here Remigius differs slightly from the philosophy of Thomas Aquinas, who posits that justice is both a part of virtue, and a virtue on its own, and therefore on par with peace as part of the *bonum communi*,[518] rather than a means by which to reach peace.

However, in a *commune* riven by dissent, justice will not always lead to peace, but can lead to further division and a continuation of conflict. Remigius acknowledges this as well. By spending much of the treatise discussing what it means for a precept, such as virtue, to have both positive and negative aspects, likening the positive aspect of justice, i.e. the punishment of wrongdoing, to the application of medical interventions by a doctor, he is able to shift focus from the strict enforcement of laws to the *bonum communi*: "In the same way he who carries out justice must consider whether the punishment results in good or in evil for the community, or the nobler part of

---

[518] *Summa Theologica* I-II, 96.3.

it."[519] This focus on the *summmum bonum* and the *bonum communi* is what ties all of these political works together. Presenting a multi faceted approach to the restoration of a unified Florence that is brought about through the sublimation of one's own private good, one's own property rights, and even the punishment of wrongdoers to the necessity of the *bonum communi.*

---

[519] Ita et illa qui facit iustitiam debet facere ut scilicet consideret si punitio redundat in bonum vel in malum communis vel nobilior parties.

The De Iustitia

by Brother Remigius dei Girolami O.P.

"Love justice you who judge the earth" as is said in *The Wisdom of Solomon*.[520] When we had written the treatise on mercy, it seemed reasonable that this offered the opportunity to speak also to some extent concerning justice, that we may discuss how much the sun of justice has granted. This is the chariot with which the Lord comes to us: as the Psalm says: "all the ways of the Lord are merciful and truthful"[521] and since it requires these that we may ascend through them to Him; according to *Proverbs*: "May mercy and truth, that is justice, never desert you, place them around your neck and inscribe them on the

---

[520] *The Wisdom of Solomon* 1:1
[521] *Psalm* 25:10

tables of your heart and you will find"[522] et cetera... Discipline, that is justice and mercy, is mostly abandoned, even if it is kept by a few here and there, as Gregory says in the *Moralia on Job.*[523] Nor is it true that one of these is contrary to the other, as it may perhaps appear in the heart since, according to the saints and philosophers, he who has one virtue has them all. Indeed, both justice and mercy are virtues. This is apparent since a virtue leads to having good and its work yields yet more good, as the philosopher says in the second book of the *Ethics.*[524] One good is not opposed to another, but to an ill and one ill to another, as wasteful extravagance is opposed to stinginess, according to the philosopher in the *Categories.*[525] This is also apparent since a virtue is an elective habit, which rests in the middle part. Oneness is the midpoint between many extremes and truth the midpoint between many falsehoods. So, for example, the true faith holds the midpoint between Arius, who posits that the Son is less than the Father, and Sabellius, who posits that He is equal to the Father and exists as the same person, certainly the Son has equality with the Father, but exists as another person. The true faith holds also the middle point between Euticius, who posits one person and one nature in Christ, and Nestorius, who posits two persons and two natures, teaching that Christ certainly exists as one person and two natures.

The wise man discovers the precepts of justice in two ways in the above phrase. In work, since it says: "justice"

---

[522] *Proverbs* 3:3

[523] Gregory *Moralia in Iob* I.3

[524] Aristotle *Nicomachean Ethics* II.1.

[525] Meant is, perhaps, Aristotle *Nicomachean Ethics* IV.1

and in working, since it says "love." This holds in two ways, that is, how it pertains to all working generally, since it says: "love," and secondly how it pertains to someone working specifically, since it says: "you who judge the earth," since these especially are to do justice. Even so the command to love pertains to everyone, should they wish to be observers of the precepts of justice, so that they do just work not because of shame or fear or desire or empty glory or friendship or parents or other inordinate reason, but for the love of justice itself. Virtue is to be loved on its own account; nevertheless, it is not to end there, but to continue into the ultimate end, that is happiness and the highest good, just as the teacher explains in the first book of the *Sentences*.[526]

The type of these precepts are twofold: on the one hand they are affirmative, which oblige one to carry them out, so the precept: "honor your father;" on the other hand some are negative, which oblige one not to do them, so the precept: "do not steal" and suchlike. A precept, however, which is given by justice encompasses both types, that is, it is able to have its designated function and its opposite. Justice, understood generally, is in the accomplishment of some good deed in whatever type and in stopping some type of falsehood, as Augustine said, that to refrain from evil and to do good are two parts of justice and so justice encompasses both types of commands. Understood in another, less general fashion, that is in the accomplishment of some good deed of whatever type, then it pertains to the affirmative type and not the negative.

---

[526] Peter the Lombard *Liber Sex Sententiarum* I.2

There is a great difference between these two types, since the negative command obliges one to obey it always and in every circumstance, whatever the person, time, place or other diverse circumstance one is in. This is so, since that which is evil by nature can in no way be made good. On the other hand, the affirmative command is to be obeyed always, but is not applicable in every circumstance depending on the urgency of the circumstance, whether in sacrifices or divine services, since these are not always to be celebrated or sung or prayed et cetera; or in rites of purification, since it is not always the time for lamentation and confession et cetera; or in prayers and other offices for the departed, since it is not always time for prayer et cetera; or in wicked deeds that must be punished, since these act similarly to medicines, according to the philosopher in the second book of the *Ethics*.[527] A physician also does not always administer a medicine after learning of an infirmity, but considers the time, for example if there is a waning quarter moon or if the dog star is in purification and so forth; and he considers the place, for example if the location is swollen or healthy, since it is good to use a diet regimen on an engorged area. Therefore, an absolute definition does not follow, according to the philosopher. Again the physician considers the person, whether they are frail or strong of complexion, whether their limbs are swollen, or the whole body is and if the limbs are noble or common, since he is able to diagnose an illness of the foot on account of the eye, but the opposite does not hold true, and to diagnose an illness of the part through an examination of the whole. In the

---

[527] Actually, in Aristotle *Nicomachean Ethics* III.5

same way he who carries out justice must consider whether the punishment results in good or in evil for the community, or the nobler part of it.

For this reason, it is necessary that many sins of the princes and of the common people are overlooked and occasionally even of the *magnati*. It is also possible that what needs to be punished in one place should not be in another place. In a city, where the populace is under domination a great man is better able to punish than elsewhere et cetera; and it is necessary sometimes to delay for various reasons, either on account of the one to be punished, or the one who is to do the punishing and other such considerations. Nothing can be considered too late which can be good, as Augustine says. This can also be understood in another way, still less generally, as befitting every virtue seeing as it is in agreement with the law. The law is double, that is innate and positive. As to the first, however, the two first precepts of justice pertain to the law; positive law too, is double, that is divine and human and thus is double justice. Divine law too is double, that is old and new, as is human law, that is civil and ecclesiastical. Civil law too is double, that is imperial and municipal.

References in the *De Iustitia*

I. Classical References

Aristotle *Nicomachean Ethics* – 195; 197

II. Old Testament References

The Wisdom of Solomon – 195
Proverbs – 195
Psalms – 195

IV. Patristic References

Gregory the Great *Moralia in Iob* – 195

V. Miscellaneous References

Peter the Lombard *Liber Sex Sententiarum* – 196

Further Reading

1.   Aquinas, Thomas *De Regno ad Regem Cypri,* Gerald Phelan (trans.) (Toronto: The Pontifical Institute for Medieval Studies, 1940).

2.   Barnes, J. Aristotle and Political Liberty. In Patzig, G. (ed.) *Aristotles' 'Politik': Akten des XI. Symposium Aristotelium, Friedrichshafen/Bodensee, 25 August – 3 September 1987* (Göttingen: Van den Hoeck und Ruprecth, 1990).

3.   Barraclough, Geoffrey. *The Medieval Papacy* (London: Thames and Hudson, 1968).

4.   Blumenthal, Uta-Renate. *The Investiture Controversy: Church and Monarchy from the Ninth to the Twelfth Century* (Philadelphia: University of Pennsylvania Press, 1988).

5.   Browning, Oscar, *Guelphs and Ghibellines: A Short History of Medieval Italy 1250-1409* (London: Methuen and Co. 1894).

6.   Brucker, G., *A Renaissance Florence* (New York: Wiley, 1969).

7.   -----------------, *Florence: The Golden Age, 1138-1737* (Berkley: University of California Press, 1998).

8.   -----------------, *Florentine Politics and Society, 1343-1378* (Princeton: Princeton University Press, 1962).

9.   ------------------, *The Civic World of Early Renaissance Florence* (Princeton: Princeton University Press, 1977).

10.   Capitani, O., L' incompiuto "tractatus de iustitia" di fra' Remigio de' Girolami (+ 1319). In *Bullettino dell' Istituto storico italiano per il Medio Evo e Archivio muratoriano* 72 (1960), pp. 91-134.

11.   Connell, William J. (ed.), *Society and Individual in Renaissance Florence* (Berkley: University of California Press, 2002).

12.   Cowdrey, H.E.J. *Popes and Church Reform in the 11th Century* (Burlington, Vermont: Ashgate, 2000).

13.   ------------------ *Pope Gregory VII, 1073-1085* (Oxford University Press, 1998).

14.   ------------------ *The Register of Pope Gregory VII, 1073-1085: an English Translation* (New York: Oxford University Press, 2002).

15.   Cross, Richards, *The Metaphysics of the Incarnation: Thomas Aquinas to Duns Scotus* (Oxford: Oxford University Press, 2002).

16.   Dameron, George, W., *Florence and its Church in the Age of Dante* (Philadelphia: University of Philadelphia Press, 2005).

17.   Davis, Charles T., *Remigio de Girolami and Dante: A Comparison of their Conception of Peace*, in *Studi Danteschi* 36 (1959).

18.　　------------------, *An Early Florentine Political Theorist: Fra Remigio de' Girolami*, in *Proceedings of the American Philosophical Society* 104.6 (American Philosophical Society, 1960), pp. 662-676.

19.　　------------------, *Education in Dante's Florence*, in *Speculum* 40.3 (Medieval Academy of America, 1965), pp. 415-435.

20.　　------------------, *Ptolemy of Lucca* and *the Roman Republic*, in *Proceedings of the American Philosophical Society* 118.1 (American Philosophical Society, 1974), pp. 30-50.

21.　　------------------, *Dante's Italy and other Essays* (Philadelphia: University of Philadelphia Press, 1984).

22.　　Egenter, *Gemeinnutz vor Eigennutz: Die soziale Leitidee im Tractatus De Bono Communi des Fr. Remigius von Florenz*, in *Scholastik* 9 (1934), pp. 79-92.

23.　　Emerton, Ephraim. *The Correspondence of Pope Gregory VI.* (New York: Columbia University Press, 1932).

24.　　Feingold, Francis, *Principium vs. Principiatum: The Transcendence of Love in Hildebrand and Aquinas*, in *Quaestiones Disputatae 3.2* (2013), pp. 56-68.

25.　　Friedman, Russell, *Dominican Quodlibetal Literature, ca.1260-1330*, in Christopher Schabel (ed.) *Theological Quodlibeta in the Middle Ages: The Fourteenth Century* (Leiden: Brill, 2007), pp. 401-492.

26.　　Friis-Jensen, *The Reception of Horace in the Middle Ages*, in Stephen Harrison (ed.) *The Cambridge Companion to*

Horace (Cambridge: Cambridge University Press, 2007), pp. 291-304.

27.   Gilchrist, John, *Simoniaca haeresis* and the problem of orders from Leo IX to Gratian. In *Proceedings of the Second International Congress of Medieval Canon Law*. C. Monumenta Iuris Canonici 1. (1965), pp. 209–235.

28.   Hankey, Wayne, Aquinas Plato and Neoplatonism. In Davies, Brian and Stump, Eleonore (edd.), *The Oxford Handbook to Aquinas* (Oxford: Oxford University Press, 2011).

29.   Henderson, Ernest F. (trans.), *Select Historical Documents of the Middle Ages* (London: George Bell and Sons, 1910).

30.   Hofmann, K. (ed.), *Der Dictatus papae Gregors VII. Eine rechtsgeschichtliche Erklärung von Dr. Theol. Karl Hofmann* (Paderborn: Ferdinand Schöningh, 1933).

31.   Kempshall, *The Common Good in Late Medieval Political Thought* (Oxford: Oxford University Press, 1999).

32.   Keys, Mary M., *Aquinas, Aristotle, and the Promise of the Common Good* (Cambridge: Cambridge University Press, 2006).

33.   Lagerlund, Erik (ed.), *Encyclopedia of Medieval Philosophy: Philosophy between 500 and 1500* (New York: Springer, 2011).

34.   Lee, Hwa-Yong, *Political Representation in the Later Middle Ages: Marsilius in Context* (New York: Peter Lang Publishing Inc., 2008).

35.   Lenzi, Vittorio, *La battaglia di Zappolino e La secchia rapita* (Edizioni il Fiorino, 1995).

36.   Leuker, Tobias, *Heiligenlob in Text und Bild. Der Hl. Dominikus und Ghirlandaios Pala für Santa Maria Novella*, in *Mitteilungen des Kunsthistorischen Institutes in Florenz* 54.3 (Florenz: Kunsthistorisches Institut in Florenz, Max-Planck-Institut, 2010-2012), pp. 425-444.

37.   Mayhew, Robert, Part and Whole in Aristotle's Political Philosophy. In *The Journal of Ethics* Vol. 1 No. 4 (1977), pp. 325-340.

38.   Malloy, Michael P, *Civil Authority in Medieval Philosophy: Lombard, Aquinas, and Bonaventure* (Lanham: University Press of America, 1985).

39.   Maritain, Jacques, *Man and the State* (Chicago: University of Chicago Press, 1951).

40.   -------------------, *The Person and the Common Good* (New York: Scribner's, 1947).

41.   Mineo, E. Igor., *Caritas* e bene commune. In *Storica* 59 XX (2014), pp. 7-56.

42.   Mäkinen, Virpi, *Property Rights in the Late Medieval Discussion on Franciscan Poverty*, in *Recherches de Théologie et Philosophie médiévales* (Leuven: Peeters, 2011).

43.   Minio-Paluello, Lorenzo, *Remigio Girolami's De Bono Communi: Florence at the Time of Dante's Banishment and the*

Philosopher's Answer to the Crisis, in *Italian Studies* 11 (1956), pp. 56-71.

44.   Morrison, Karl F. *The Investiture Controversy: Issues, Ideals and Results* (New York: Winston Inc, 2005).

45.   Murphy, Edward F. St. Thomas' Political Doctrine and Democracy. (Cleveland, Ohio: John T. Zubal, 1983).

46.   Najemy, J.M., *A History of Florence 1200-1575* (Malden: Blackwell Publishing, 2006).

47.   Ottman, H., *Geschichte des politischen Denkens: Das Mittelalter* (Stuttgart: Verlag J.B. Metzler, 2004).

48.   Panella, E., *Per lo studio di Fra. Remigio dei Girolami (†1319): "contra falsos ecclesie professores' c.c. 5-37*, (Memorie Dominicane, 1979).

49.   -----------, *Remigiana: Note biografiche e filologiche*, in *Libro e imagine* (Memorie Dominicane, 1982), pp. 366-421.

50.   -----------, *I quodlibeti di Remigio dei Girolami* (Memorie Domincane, 1983), pp. 1-149.

51.   -----------, *Nuova cronologia Remigiana*, in *Archivum Fratrum Praedicatorum* 60 (1990), pp. 145-311.

52.   --------- (ed. and trans.), *Remigio dei Girolami, Dal bene commune al bene del commune: I trattati politici di Remigio dei Girolami (†1319) nella Firenze dei bianchi-neri De bono communi – De bono pacis – Sermones de pace*, in *Biblioteca di Memorie Dominicane* 9 (Firenze: Edizioni Nerbini, 2014).

53.   Post, Gaines, *Studies in Medieval Legal Thought: Public Law and the State 1100-1322* (Princeton: Princeton University Press, 1964).

54.   Quinn, John F., *The Historical Constitution of St. Bonaventure's Philosophy* (Toronto: The Potifical Institute on Mediaeval Studies, 1973).

55.   Rice, Eugene F., *The Humanist Idea of Christian Antiquity: Lefèvre d'Étaples and his Circle*, in *Studies in the Renaissance* 9 (Chicago: University of Chicago Press, 1962), pp. 126-160.

56.   Robinson, I.S., Pope Gregory VII, the Princes and Pactum. In *The English Historical Review*. Vol.94,No.373(Oct. 1979) 721-756.

57.   Rubinstein, Nicolai (ed.), *Florentine Studies: Politics and Society in Renaissance Florence* (London: Faber, 1968).

58.   Rupers, Michael J., "Dante's Hidden Sin - Wrath: How Dante Vindictively Used The Inferno Against Contemporaries" (2016). Master's Theses and Capstone Projects. 214.

59.   Rupp, *'Common' = 'Of the Commune:' Private Property and Individualism in Remigio dei Girolami's De Bono Pacis*, in *History of Political Though* 14.1 (1993), pp. 41-56.

60.   ------, *Damnation, Individual and Community in Remigio dei Girolami's De Bono Communi*, in *History of Political Thought* 21.2 (2000), pp. 217-236.

61.   Smalley, Beryl, *Sallust in the Middle Ages*, in Bolgar, R.R. (ed.) *Classical Influences on European Culture, A.D. 500-1500* (Cambridge: Cambridge University Press, 1971), pp. 165-194.

62.   Steel, Carlos G, Guldentops, Guy and Beullens, Pieter, *Aristotle's Animals in the Middle Ages and Renaissance* (Ithaca, NY: Cornell University Press, 1999).

63.   Taylor, Henry Osborn, *The Medieval Mind: A History of the Development of Thought and Emotion in the Middle Ages Volumes I and II* (London: MacMillan and Co, 1927).

64.   Tierney, Brian, Donald Kagen, and L. Pearce Williams (eds.), *Gregory VII-Church Reformer or World Monarch?* (New York: Random House Inc, 1967).

65.   --------------- *The Middle Ages: Sources of Medieval History, Sixth edition* (New York: McGrawHill, Inc. 1999).

66.   Ullmann, Walter, *A Short History of the Papacy in the Middle Ages* (Methuen & CO LTD 1972).

67.   Weigel, Peter, *Aquinas on Simplicity: An Investigation into the Foundation of His Philosophical Theology* (Bern: Peter Lang AG, 2008).

68.   Whitney, J.P., Gregory VII. In *The English Historical Review*. Vol. 34, No.134 (Apr. 1919) 129-151

69.   Wilken, Robert, Gregory VII and the Politics of the Spirit. In *First Things; A Monthly Journal of Religious and Public Life*. Vol. 89 (1999) 26-32

70.   Williams, Schafer, *The Gregorian Epoch: Reformation, Revolution, Reaction?* (Boston: D.C. Heath and Co., 1964).

71.   Wilmot-Buxton, Ethel, *The Story of Hildebrand, St. Gregory VII* (New York: P.J. Kenedy & Sons. 1920).

99052237R00127

Made in the USA
Lexington, KY
13 September 2018